shift

Innovation That Disrupts Markets, Topples Giants, and Makes You #1

JAGAN NEMANI

DEDICATION

To my lovely wife and kids, who missed me a lot
during the time I was working on this book.

Contents

Acknowledgments

Never did I dream that I would actually write a book. I was happy blogging about my experiences, but many of my friends and acquaintances saw the potential and motivated me to take this journey. I would not have started without their support; hence, a grateful acknowledgment is due to all of them.

A good coach has a big impact on an individual's work, especially when that individual is taking on a task for the first time. We all know of the impact good coaches have on athletes, with marathon runners and in the gym; little did I know that this is applicable to writing as well. My coach, Dr. Liz Alexander, has had an immense impact on me, my writing style, and the contents of this book. She is a tough coach who did not let me cut corners or compromise on quality. She holds herself to a high standard and ensured that I delivered content that met that standard. Without her support, I would have written a good textbook, but now I believe I have written a book that my target audience can truly enjoy. I cannot thank Dr. Liz enough for nudging me to do the right thing, motivating me and supporting me throughout this journey — in short, for coaching me well.

Ambal Balakrishnan is the core conspirator behind this book. She is a good friend who saw the potential in me and took on the task of convincing me to write this book. Numerous phone calls and long discussions later, I was certain that I *had* to write a book on a topic that I am passionate about. Little did I know that she was signing me up for a multi-year project! Nonetheless, I would not have taken this path, let alone completed it, without her support. Thanks, Ambal, for your persistence and for recognizing the author within me.

It is very challenging to understand the inner workings of any industry, especially if you have not spent time in that industry. I have never worked in the pharmaceutical industry, but I was curious to see if my customer experience framework has any relevance in that setting. So I reached out to Purnanand Sarma, President and CEO of Taris Biomedical, to discuss my ideas. He gave me a good run down on the history of the industry, how it had changed over decades, and the direction the industry is headed — something only a true industry expert can share. We discussed the framework and he gave examples that support it; discussions with him gave me the insights I needed to start conducting my research about the industry. During my research, I talked to physicians and pharmacists to understand patient characteristics further, and was able to show how this industry strives to deliver better customer experience. I owe my research and knowledge on the pharmaceutical industry to Purnanand, and he has my heartfelt thanks for his support.

Throughout this book, I have provided specific examples of innovative companies delivering the desired customer experience to shift the market. Though much of the data presented in this book is publicly available, the true stories behind the data come from the leaders of these businesses. Kevin Goodwin, the CEO of Sonosite; Ivan Braiker, the co-founder/CEO of Hipcricket; and Noah Spitzer Williams, the founder/CEO of Highlight Hunter, were gracious enough to meet with me and share their stories of starting a company and building it by focusing on customer experience. All of them are very passionate leaders who care for their customers and the topic of customer experience. Thank you, Kevin, Ivan and Noah, for your support and for helping with my research on this book.

Sandeep Krishnamurthy, director of the University of Washington-Bothell School of Business, made a significant contribution towards this book. His was the first business validation of my customer experience framework. We had a long discussion of the framework, and at the end he asked me to write a book on the topic. By then, I had started down the path of writing the book, but it was a good validation coming from a business professor. He also helped me think though some of the gaps in the concept and made introductions to some key executives. Thank you, Sandeep, for providing the motivation to write this book through your validation and support.

Independent authors need the right support network to become successful. Such a network was provided to me by Dr. Liz, who introduced me to some of the amazing people I have worked throughout the journey. Lauryl Eddlemon designed a beautiful cover for the book that conveyed its message in a beautiful way. Leonard Pierce helped with copyediting and making the book easy to read. Sandeep Bhandaru, who is a good friend, and has helped me with his artistic abilities. Sriya Nemani, who did a great job proofreading the book and helped me avoid some expensive mistakes..

Next is a group of people I call my 'advisory board', which consists of successful executives who met with me, discussed my framework; and provided good feedback. This helped me think through the concepts further and articulate them in a better way. Thank you, Luis Salazar, Sajal Sahay and Sharath Dorbala, for providing such great input; you have helped me improve the overall quality of the book.

Last but not the least is the Startup Leadership Program (SLP) and its fellows. They are a group of smart entrepreneurs who have helped me with my research and a few of my stories. Thank you for all the feedback and making sure that I write a book that is relevant to you all.

Introduction

In early 2009 — it seemed like a good idea at the time — I quit my job as a management consultant at Deloitte, one of the biggest corporate strategy firms in the world, and launched my own energy-efficiency start-up. After all, three things had aligned to make me believe I was on the verge of something big — very big indeed.

First, I had amassed considerable experience that suggested there was a huge need for what I had to offer. During the three years I had been in management consulting, I'd become very interested in the cleantech industry — specifically, educating myself about "solar space", which is everything related to the manufacturing, distribution and installation of solar panels for the purpose of generating electricity. After talking to a number of solar energy experts, I had gained sufficient knowledge to become the resident solar industry expert within Deloitte. As part of my job as a solar industry expert, I had to develop strategic viewpoints on the future of the industry. One of my findings, through research and interviews, was that solar was unlikely to meet more than one percent of U.S. energy needs; the electricity demand of most homes/offices far exceeded what could be generated on their rooftops using solar. This meant that distributed energy generation, whereby electricity is generated on rooftops across the country using technologies like solar, was far from becoming a reality.

One of the main roadblocks to distributed energy generation was energy efficiency. Most homes in the United States waste about 45 percent energy, while offices and other commercial establishments waste an even higher percentage. If we could cut down on electricity wasted at these locations by improving their energy efficiency, then their total electricity demand would go down — and with a lower demand for electricity, solar would be able to generate enough electricity to meet that demand.

Nevertheless, there was one major hurdle — human behavior. Energy wastage in United States is a bad habit that people have developed over the years. Low electricity tariffs do not incentivize people to save energy, and saving energy is not considered sexy or fashionable; rather the opposite is often true as malls and other public places continue to use lights to build ambience. We've all seen them: the empty office buildings where lights remain on 24/7; houses with porch lights on during daylight hours; department stores lit up like Christmas trees well beyond their operating hours; and electronics outlets where all the TV monitors remain blaring even when no one is around to watch them.

The second alignment came into play due to active carbon footprint education delivered by many non-profit organizations like the Environmental Defense Fund (EDF). Al Gore's documentary *An Inconvenient Truth* shed light on global warming issues and the impact they could have on our future. Many other Non-Governmental Organizations (NGOs) had taken up the task of educating people on the perils of carbon emissions; big, innovative companies like HP, Intuit, BT, SAP, Deloitte, Apple, Pepsi, and General Electric, to name a few, had taken on initiatives to measure and reduce their carbon footprints. Many companies had green champions, whose goal was to educate the organization about ways to reduce carbon emissions.

Though there was positive momentum around carbon emissions measurement and reduction, there was increasing skepticism as well. Many believed there was not much truth to the entire global warming story. They feared that any type of carbon emissions control would end up taxing individuals and businesses, and cripple the economy further.

But then the third alignment came into play, as newly elected President Barack Obama included a "cap-and-trade" proposal in his first budget. This proposal put restrictions on pollution that causes global warming and provided companies an option to pay for the "right to pollute". All corporations were given a certain amount of carbon credits (i.e., the right to pollute), and if they polluted more than their pre-assigned limits they would have to buy more credits from the market. Many corporations started preparing themselves for this regulation by cutting down their energy usage. Though the proposal had a long way to go to become a law, if it passed, it would help the business model I was developing. Once this regulation was in place, it would discourage corporations and their employees from wasting energy, forcing them to change their behavior. As more and more people looked at ways of changing their habits and saving energy, my startup would help them in their mission.

It appeared the time was right to get into the market of helping people change their habits by providing them with a website where they could join communities, benchmark their energy usage, and save energy together. The idea for my start-up was taking form.

Market research suggested that people liked saving energy in communities of likeminded people who could motivate and nudge them to save energy. It also suggested that people wanted to compare their energy usage against others in their community, and be part of regular challenges for saving energy — and they wanted to do this for free.

So I planned on building a website where people could create their own online community, inviting other users from work, friends circle, church, neighborhood, or anywhere else to join them. They could then benchmark their energy (both electricity and gas) usage against others, set up savings challenges, get relevant tips, and save energy together in the community. This social website would be built to help people change their energy usage behaviors, using peer pressure and other social nudges.

As for the business model, I was planning to offer my website's services for free, and sell users solar equipment and other energy-efficiency products in bulk. I would also create strategic alliances with companies, offering my website's services to create work communities focused on saving energy. This would help the companies increase employee engagement with green initiatives. The energy usage behavior change that would result as part of this service would help companies cut down their energy usage — and hence their carbon footprint.

My startup started out well, as I got plenty of attention from big companies. I was attending environmental conferences where people were excited to see my prototype and provided a lot of positive feedback. I was busy interacting with companies, their employees, and individual users, and was looking forward to closing my first deal with a major company.

I was also talking with local non-profits who were helping homeowners save energy. Their interaction with these homeowners was one-off; they'd meet with them once and give them some energy-saving tips and some CFL bulbs. But they could not sustain a longer-term relationship with homeowners. Using my website, they could enroll homeowners into an online community and increase their long-term interaction with them.

My idea was further validated when Microsoft entered the market with their Hohm website, which was similar to mine but focused on helping individuals save energy. They also measured the energy usage of those individuals, gave them targeted tips, and helped them in saving energy. They had exactly the same focus that I had, with some significant differences:

- I was focused on communities, while they were focused on individuals.
- Microsoft had millions of dollars to spend on marketing, while I was tweeting energy saving tips every day in the hope of gaining attention.
- Big utility companies were willing to work with Microsoft and provide individuals' energy usage data. The local non-profits that partnered with me wanted me to pay them for using my service.

Nevertheless, Microsoft's entry into the market gave this issue much-required attention and hope for a largely ignored facet of energy efficiency.

There was one further depressing similarity between Microsoft's Hohm and my site — neither of us succeeded. My website was taken down in July 2010, after I burned through my cash and ran out of runway, waiting for user traffic to pick up. Microsoft Hohm was shut down in May 2012. According to their website, even though they had encouraging feedback from customers and partners, slow market adoption of the service caused them to shut it down. I had spent thousands of dollars in building the technology and on marketing my website, while Microsoft had spent millions. Regardless, neither of us was able to excite sufficient users to save energy by using our online tools to save energy.

Where had we gone wrong? Why was it so difficult to get consumers and businesses to save energy and benefit the environment by cutting back on carbon emissions?

The answer to this question lies in the customer experience delivered by these energy-saving solutions. They were not convenient to use and forced users to change their behaviors — something that is very difficult to do. For example, one of the energy-saving tips was to reduce phantom power loss due to the unused chargers and electronics that are left plugged in through the night. The best way to reduce phantom power loss is to unplug these chargers and electronics. Now imagine a family of five who have 6 rooms containing chargers and electronics throughout the house. It would be a big undertaking for the parents to make sure everything was unplugged before they go to bed; they might do it for a day or two, but it would be pretty easy for them to fall back into their usual habits.

There are more such examples. It is easier for us to leave the porch light on than to get out of the bed, go downstairs, and turn it off. It feels more secure and easy to leave the lights on inside a store at night than to turn them off. Moreover, with cheap electricity rates, the cost of wasting energy is not high, so there is no incentive for users to take on the inconvenient tasks for saving energy.

From a customer experience point of view, saving energy, when done manually, is very inconvenient, and when it's done using technology, it can get pretty expensive. So the bottom line impact of trying to save energy is minimal and not immediate. On top of that, using a website to measure and benchmark energy usage, read tips, and implement those tips is over-the-top inconvenient. It is not surprising, then, that sites like mine and Microsoft's Hohm that have focused on these ideas have failed to attract enough customers. We focused on innovation from the perspective of technology, not how the customer would experience that technology.

This failure taught me never to ignore the customer experience when launching innovative initiatives, so that expensive innovation mistakes can be avoided.

Having learned this important lesson, I was ready to test it out in the market, and I was fortunate enough to have gotten my job back at Deloitte as a management consultant. I started back and tested this new learning with some of my clients, and what I found was amazing. Every time my client focused on customer experience right from the outset and adjusted their offering, business model, pricing, and internal processes to deliver the right customer experience, the results were astonishing, but whenever they ignored the customer experience, the results were dismal.

Armed with this knowledge and experience, I started researching customer experience-driven innovation and the impact it has on investment returns. To keep it industry-agnostic, I researched successful companies from the technology, medical devices, banking, and pharmaceuticals industries — companies that were serving consumers (B2C) as well as those that were selling to businesses (B2B). After studying close to 40 companies and their innovative practices, I found that companies that focus on delivering a better customer experience are able to achieve better business results, irrespective of the industry they operate in or the type of customers they serve.

Companies like Netflix have been able to bankrupt billion-dollar incumbents like Blockbuster. Startups like Fab.com have been able to attract over two million customers in less than seven months, in an overcrowded e-commerce industry. Zappos.com was able to build and sell shoes to customers online, while its brick and mortar competitors struggled to keep their stores open. Hipcricket was able to dominate the mobile advertising and marketing industry by using its combination of product and consulting services. Sonosite was able to create a new product category of hand carrier ultrasound machines, even after Philips and other industry veterans wrote off this innovative company. Pharmaceutical companies have been able to charge a 90 percent price premium and still quadruple their drug sales. Details about these companies and the innovation returns realized by them are shared throughout this book.

Based on my research, I have developed a nine-factor customer experience framework that is applicable to most industries. This framework can be used to understand the requirements of your target customer segments and the experience currently delivered by the market incumbents. Based on this understanding, you can find gaps with the desired customer experience and build a successful business by satisfying the needs of your customers. Throughout this book, you will discover how many of these successful companies delivered best-in-class customer experience on some of the same factors to shift the market in their favor. They used this approach to successfully dominate their markets, even under the most adverse market conditions.

Innovation should not be hard; companies should not have to lose so much of their Research & Development (R&D) investment; and innovators should be able to succeed more often. This can be achieved through customer experience-driven innovation, which is the focus of this book.

Much has been written about customer experience, and there is no end of information about innovation. This book uniquely blends both together, along with an innovative customer experience framework. It is structured to share the experiences of other successful companies in a way that will help you disrupt the market, topple giants and become #1 — in short, shift the market. Each chapter is structured to help you understand the importance of innovating using the customer experience framework prescribed in this book.

Chapter 1 discusses the importance of the customer experience, and how this has become the essential ingredient for many innovation methodologies. Proliferation of technology and information has made it easier for customers to learn about different solutions, to compare them against the kinds of experiences they need, and, based on that, to choose the right solution. There are innovators who see this empowerment of the customer as an opportunity, and develop solutions to cater to those needs. That is why customer experience has become such an important driver.

In Chapter 2, I introduce a customer experience framework and the nine factors that define it for both B2B and B2C customers. I developed this framework to graphically depict the importance of customer experience factors. My research, my experience with innovation and solving customer problems, and the experiences of many leaders who have led successful innovation initiatives are the foundation of this framework. I have used it in my interviews with many such successful innovators across different industries, and many of their success stories fit well into the framework.

In Chapters 3 through 6, I use the customer experience framework to explain the recent successes of innovation initiatives across different industries. You will find examples from consumer-focused companies thriving in an overcrowded market, business focused-companies stealing share from market leaders, startups creating a new product category in unfavorable markets, and drug companies changing their focus every few years to deliver best customer experience. All of these examples show how companies were able to shift the market by focusing on certain aspects of customer experience that were ignored by the incumbent giants. This will help you understand how the entire framework works together beyond just the individual elements, so you can analyze your own business situations to shift the market by delivering best-in-class customer experience.

Chapter 7 outlines different types of innovation and how they were used to deliver best-in-class customer experience. Once you have a clear understanding of the desired customer experience, you need the right type of innovation to deliver it. In this chapter we discuss the three different types of innovation — business model innovation, process innovation and product innovation — that successful companies have used, individually or in combination, to deliver best-in-class customer experience. This doesn't happen by accident, as you will later discover.

If you are an entrepreneur or innovation-focused leader, you will find this book useful in helping you understand and evaluate the requirements of your target customer segment. You can then use that understanding to innovate and create a stronger market position for yourself. The deeper understanding of your customer and the experience they demand will help you increase your focus in terms of reaching and serving those customers. The book will provide you with the tools that will assist you in disrupting the market, toppling the giants and becoming #1.

· **CHAPTER 1** ·

Why Customer Experience?

I t was Christmas day in 2009, and Trevor was very excited about the GoPro camera he got as a gift. GoPro cameras are wearable, gear-mountable, waterproof, versatile cameras that enable active sports enthusiasts to record quality videos of their athletic endeavors. Trevor was in his early twenties, and wanted to record his cool snowboarding stunts. He called his best friend Noah right away to share this news, as both had been wanting to shoot snowboarding videos for a long time. The pair was extremely eager, and made big plans for the winter sport season ahead.

Trevor and Noah had a great time recording videos of all the tricks they did on their snowboards, like the back flip at the terrain park or the 50-50 slide. There were some funny moments, as well, like when they wiped out on a big jump and fell flat on their faces.

At the end of the season, Noah asked Trevor to make a highlight video to share with their friends on YouTube. Trevor laughed at the idea; he didn't want to go over hundreds of hours of video just to make something worth sharing with his friends. Soon, Trevor and Noah's excitement about the GoPro camera and all the videos they'd recorded fizzled. They tried many different video editing software products available in the market; though these products offered great editing and enhancing functionality, none of them could help them find highlights within their videos. So they gave up the idea of making the summary video and went back to their regular routines.

In May 2010, they decided to go on a kite boarding trip. So they geared up for their trip, grabbed the GoPro camera and recorded all their cool tricks. When they got back home, they had several hours of video, but again, there was no way to find the highlights in the footage. This was extremely frustrating to Trevor and Noah, so they decided to build their own solution for easily picking out highlights from a video stream.

They started off by brainstorming about the key customer experience requirements that would be crucial for such a solution. First, it should be able to pick out highlights, like action shots, from hours of video footage; their estimate was that there would be two to five minutes of highlights in any one hour of video. Second, they should not incur any additional hardware costs to use the solution. This meant that the solution should work with whatever camera they currently had and should not need additional hardware like a remote control. Most people wear gloves during active sports, so the third requirement was that the solution should work while wearing gloves. Since most people realize that they have something worthwhile after shooting a video, the highlight is usually present before the user tags the video; so this became the final requirement — that highlight-tagging be done after the shot is complete. Because they were the customers of this solution, they were able to clearly articulate its requirements.

Now, the two started brainstorming ways to meet the necessary requirements. The user had to have some way to tag the video immediately after recording something cool without using any additional hardware. This is when they had a bright idea: the user would have to cover the lens of the camera with their hands to tag the video. This would create dark frames in the video stream which can be searched and retrieved. Additionally, covering of the lens works well even with gloves on, so this helped them meet their final requirement.

Next, they had to figure out how to build the solution. This is when they ran into their next major problem: neither knew much about coding editing software. After a few hours of brainstorming (and a few beers), they hit an insurmountable wall — or so they thought.

In September 2010, Noah was still frustrated because there was no solution to find highlights in his video. So he started searching the web for ways to build a solution; soon, he'd found some open source components he could stitch together to build a prototype. He spent a day learning about them and how to make them work together, and within 24 hours he had a functional prototype of the solution. He wanted to test it right away, so he and his girlfriend went out paddleboarding, and the entire time, he kept covering the lens to tag highlights within the video stream. After couple of hours, he returned home and uploaded the video into his prototype — and was thrilled to see that it worked. He found all the highlights he had tagged in the video. He was amazed that by spending 24 hours of his personal time, he could build a solution he could not find in any professional video editing software products. This encouraged him to build the solution out further — and maybe to start his own company.

Over the next year, Noah kept exploring the possibility of starting his own company focused on selling the highlight-hunting software. In August 2011, he met with executives at a camera company; they liked his approach and suggested that he should start his own business. By September, Noah had quit his comfortable job at Microsoft to start "Highlight Hunter". Up until this point, he had invested less than $10,000, but quite a bit of his time. He was about to find out if he could get any traction with the software solution he had developed.

Further validation for his solution came when the video production team at GoPro started using his software to find highlights in their videos. This twelve-member team's job is to shoot videos that can be used for marketing GoPro cameras, so they go to sporting events and shoot videos using an average of 20 cameras. Once they complete shooting, they go back to their hotel rooms and scan through over 50 hours of video to find those golden nuggets for marketing their cameras. This process of scanning the videos, finding the golden nuggets and editing them for marketing purposes once took them about 15 hours, and was extremely laborious; using Highlight Hunter software, the team was able to shave off six hours from their processing time, at a significant cost saving for GoPro.

Though Highlight Hunter is still an early-stage startup, Noah has been able to meet the unmet needs of a specific customer segment. To date he has invested less than $30,000 and lots of time into his company, but even with such small investment, he has created a solution that many of the big video software companies, with their big development budgets, have not been able to deliver.

New Innovation Paradigm

Noah is not an outlier, and definitely not the only one building solutions to solve specific pain points. There are many such innovators who are able to cater to the unmet needs of a customer with minimal investment. These innovators are not afraid of saturated markets or big incumbents with deep pockets; instead, they focus on unsatisfied customers with unmet needs and look to build their businesses around serving them in the best possible way.

Many of these innovators believe in the "Lean Startup[1]" methodology and attend "Startup Weekend[2]" sessions. Eric Ries introduced the Lean Startup in his best selling book of the same name; it aims at changing the way products are developed at any company by preaching a newer innovation approach: learning about customer requirements, validating them with rapid prototypes and iteratively developing the product with active customer feedback.

Startup Weekend puts the Lean Startup approach into practice. It's Just what it sounds like: a 54-hour weekend event that starts on Friday night and goes on until Sunday evening. During this time, groups of developers, business managers, designers, marketing gurus, and anyone else interested in startups form teams and work on developing an idea. Throughout the weekend, these innovators work diligently on understanding the requirements of their customers, defining the solution, building a working prototype, and testing the solution in the market. At the end of the weekend, they present their solution and its business case to the panelists. As of October 2012, 672 such weekend events have been conducted in over 300 cities in 100 countries, attended by 57,000 innovators and leading to the creation of 5,000 startups[3].

Both these methodologies put the customer at the center of innovation, and they do so because they have learned from experience that delivering best-in-class customer experience is the best way to win in the present economy. Today's customers have way too much choice, and access to lots

---

[1] http://theleanstartup.com/
[2] http://startupweekend.org/
[3] http://en.wikipedia.org/wiki/Startup_Weekend

of information — and they use that information to find a solution that meets their requirements. If you are part of the retail or electronics industries, you know that customer loyalty is a thing of the past. Customers do not mind shopping around to find the solution that meets all their needs. This creates opportunities for new entrants to deliver best-in-class customer experience to them and win their business.

Throughout this book you will find plentiful examples of companies that have put the customer at the center of their innovation, and figured out ways to deliver best-in-class customer experience; those customers have responded by giving them increased sales and market share. You will also read about customers helping these innovators create a new product category within a closed market, like the radiology equipment market. They have helped companies become market leaders and bankrupt incumbents, and they have helped ensure that these innovators are successful. Without them, the customers would be unable to enjoy a better customer experience.

Why is this a new innovation paradigm?

For many years, big companies have followed the methodology of "build it and they will come". They focused on hiring visionaries who could come up with bright ideas; then they would throw their war chest at these ideas, build the products for years, and launch them to the market. Seldom did these companies consult with their customers or do market testing to see if their innovation would be successful. In cases where they *did* consult, they would go away for years to build the products, only to realize that customer needs had changed over that time. More often than not, these innovations failed in the market. According to research done by innovation consulting group Doblin (part of Monitor Consulting), about 96 percent of all innovation attempts fail to meet their performance targets. This is because what these innovators *thought* the market needed and what it *actually* needed were drastically different.

This is not the case with just new or disruptive innovation. The closed-door methodology is even used for incrementally improving the products. Even today, there are product managers who seldom visit a customer, who have never seen a customer use their products, and who have never bothered to understand the reasons behind customer attrition. They think they know what customers want, because they have been reviewing requests filed with support; but when asked to explain the motivations behind a customer request, they start making assumptions and drawing conclusions, many of which are completely wrong. Still, these product managers come up with beautiful product roadmaps and strategy presentations — not grounded in the reality of customer experience, but built on their own assumptions. Companies that still innovate behind closed doors and with minimal customer input open opportunities for innovators to disrupt the market.

The innovators are able to make the best use of such opportunities because of their customer-centric approach to innovation. They do not believe in spending a lot of time or money on opportunities that fail to yield good results, so they use all means of customer research available — like internet research, online surveys, coffee shop interviews, and mobile marketing campaigns. The focus of this research is to uncover any unmet needs or learn about bad experiences customers have had using certain products.

Once these innovators have learned about the opportunities, they do not go back behind closed doors to build the ideal product; rather, they build a prototype to further test the market providing them more customer input which helps in improving the product. They then launch a minimal viable product — a product that delivers just enough functionality to excite the users. When customers start using this product, which is often buggy and incomplete, the innovators learn from them what is important and what is not. Based on this information, they improve the product so as to meet the customer needs. By following this iterative approach of gathering customer feedback along the way offering fixes, they ensure that they have developed a product that meets the most important customer requirements.

Furthermore, most entrepreneurs are pretty smart about the way they build the product in the first place. If we consider the example of tech start-ups, they do not go about buying servers and writing code from scratch. As buying, operating and maintaining a server farm requires significant investment and writing code from scratch requires substantial time commitment. These practices could cost a great deal of money and time, and entrepreneurs are not guaranteed to recover their investment if they take this approach. Instead, they buy some server space from Amazon Web Services for a minimal monthly payment, and find open source code that they can stitch together to make their solution. By using this approach, the entrepreneurs are able to get to market fast with minimal investment.

The entrepreneurs and innovators who use this new paradigm of innovation pose a real threat to the incumbents, who tend to ignore the requirements of their customers; and the bigger problem is that these threats do not even show up on the incumbent's radar until they have gathered considerable traction from their customers. By the time they show up, it is often too late.

This is the power of customer experience-driven innovation — something many of the incumbents of today do not understand, and that innovators can exploit.

Customer Experience is Essential

Poet and author Maya Angelou inadvertently made the best pitch for customer experience[4] :

"People will forget what you said

People will forget what you did

But people will never forget how you made them feel."

This is the essence of customer experience-driven innovation, and the focus of this book. If you meet your customer needs and they enjoy the experience they get from using your products and services, you leave them no reason to try anyone else's offering. When that is not the case, there are unsatisfied customers looking for viable alternatives, and that opens the window of opportunity for innovators.

The target audience for this book are innovators and entrepreneurs, so I will not focus on ways for incumbents to save their market. Instead, I want to focus on ways innovators have used these opportunities to deliver a better customer experience. This book contains ample illustrations of innovative companies delivering best-in-class customer experience and shifting the market in their favor; they explain the underlying dynamics of the customer experience, and the ways the innovators have leveraged them to shift the market.

The innovative customer experience framework introduced in the next chapter can be your starting point in defining the right customer experience. This framework lays out the different aspects of customer experience

---

[4] http://www.brainyquote.com/quotes/quotes/m/mayaangelo392897.html

in an easy-to-understand visual format. Using the framework, you can map the experience *delivered* by the different players serving your customer; you should also map the experience *desired* by your customers on this framework. Based on this mapping, you should clearly see the unmet needs of your customer segment, and covering this gap should be the focus of your innovation.

· **CHAPTER 2** ·

Customer Experience Framework

Bef, efore we jump into the details of the customer experience framework, let us quickly see what a bad customer experience looks like.

Imagine you are the owner of a small startup in San Francisco, and are traveling to Philadelphia for an important customer meeting. You make travel reservations online, including an economy airfare with a stopover in Chicago, a rental car, and a hotel. You have a daylong customer meeting, so you plan on reaching Philadelphia the night before and flying back home after your meeting. You use a rental car coupon to get an upgrade, and a deeply discounted prepaid hotel for one night.

On your travel day, the weather in San Francisco is bad and your flight to Chicago is delayed by an hour and a half. This puts your trip at risk, as the connection time in Chicago is only an hour and you might miss your flight to Philadelphia. You board the flight, hoping to somehow make your connection.

Your hopes are dashed as your connecting flight, the last of the day to Philadelphia, leaves without you. The airline company books you on the first flight the next morning, but refuses to provide any accommodation. Given that the flight delay was due to bad weather, and they do not provide accommodation under such circumstances. Since you're stuck in Chicago for the night, you try to figure out your options; you want to look your best for the customer meeting, so you find a cheap hotel close to the airport and hope to get a good night's sleep.

Before you settle down, however, you call the hotel in Philadelphia to cancel your reservation. The hotel staff appreciates your letting them know about the unexpected change, but is unwilling to refund your money, as you have a prepaid reservation. After a long argument, you hang up the phone; this has been a lousy day with two bad customer experiences (airlines and hotel).

Lying in bed, you can't help but think about your day. You've decided that you will never fly with this airline again, or book any more rooms with the hotel chain, even if they are the best deals available. The poor customer experiences have convinced you that they are not worth the savings.

The next morning, your flight from Chicago to Philadelphia is uneventful, but when you get to the rental car agent, you find that your reservation has been cancelled. You explain the situation, and they rent you a similar car with a GPS. You are in a hurry to make it to your customer meeting, so you do not check the contract. Once you are close to your customer's office you try to call them to get the exact location, but your cell phone has no signal. So you pull into one of the buildings and use a landline; you get directions to your customer's location and are glad when you finally make it to the meeting.

You have a great meeting, but when you return the rental car, you are surprised by the charges: three times the amount on the original contract. The coupon you used was valid for online car reservations only; since that reservation was cancelled by the rental company, and you made a new one at the rental location, the coupon is no longer valid. Additionally, the GPS that you thought was free was actually charged at $14.99 per day. You try to get the charges reversed to your original estimate, but the car rental company does not agree. Since you're at risk of missing your flight back home, you decide to fight it out later.

In this example, we see a lot of bad customer experiences delivered by the airline, hotel, car rental company, and even the cell phone service provider. Most of us have had such bad customer experiences — maybe not all at once — and after every such experience we make a resolution not to do business with the company any more, but due to a lack of better alternatives we end up returning. When there is a viable alternative, however, the companies lose our business — and likely the business of any friends with whom we decide to share our horror stories.

Throughout this book, we will evaluate such poor customer experiences and uncover how innovators shift the market away from the incumbents by better focusing on the needs of a specific customer segment. It is with the promise of a better customer experience that innovators provide a compelling reason for customers to try their products or services, and once the customer tries their offering and has a better experience, they tend to bring in even more business by sharing their experience with others, writing positive reviews online, providing recommendations, and spreading the word about a better alternative. As the word spreads, the innovator starts gaining more of the market share, displacing the incumbent from its strong position and shifting the market in their favor. In some extreme cases they may even put the incumbent out of business. This is how a customer experience-driven innovation shifts the market and creates new leaders.

So how do you identify a poor customer experience? We surely know it when we have experienced one, but how might we know if it would open up opportunities for us as an innovator?

To understand this, we need to know what drives good as well as poor customer experiences. We need a framework for systematically researching and understanding customer experiences and their related pain points.

Over the years, I have worked with many companies that sell to other businesses (B2B) as well as to consumers (B2C). Most of them think about the customer experience as just customer service, and make an effort to improve that service. But true customer experience is much more than that, and it starts well before the customer does business with the company. It starts with the company's strategic priorities, design of its product or service, development of its business model, and hiring and training of its employees. In short, everything that a company does has an impact on the customer experience, including its people, culture, products and business practices.

I would define the customer experience as "the overall customer perception formed by interaction with the tangible and intangible assets of a company, like brand, employees, product, services, IT systems and policies." This broad definition makes it clear that everything the company does has an impact on its customer experience. It is therefore not easy to get better at delivering good customer experience, especially if it is not in your company's DNA. So how can we deconstruct this complex and challenging problem into smaller actionable factors we can act on to improve customer experience?

Through my research and work with innovative companies on challenging problems, I have found that nine factors drive the majority of the customer experiences. Everything that a company demonstrates is a good or poor experience across these nine factors, and sets the tone for the overall customer experience.

Figure 1 shows a "**Customer Experience Framework**" with nine key factors: Requirements; Price; Availability; Convenience; Service/Support;

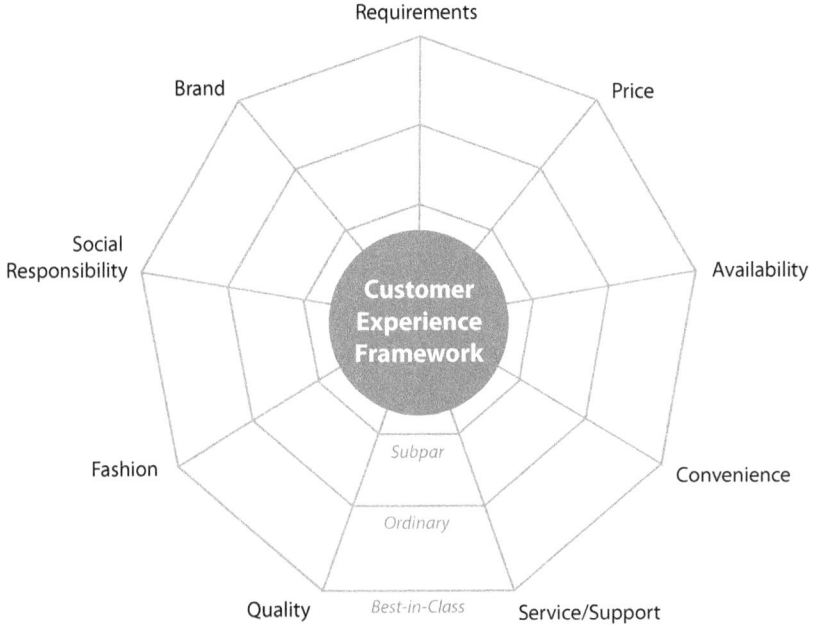

Figure 1: Customer Experience Framework

Quality; Fashion; Social Responsibility and Brand. The combination of these nine factors drives the right experience for all customer segments. I have researched companies across many different industries, and can confirm that these nine factors deliver the optimal customer experience across the board. In this book, you will see examples of how the actions of a company in any industry will manifest as the customer experience across these nine factors.

Companies from technology, telecommunications, healthcare, pharmaceuticals, banking, retail, insurance and many other industries deliver either "Best-in-class", "Ordinary" or "Subpar" customer experience across these nine factors. An innovator's goal should be to differentiate themselves by delivering a better experience across three of the nine factors that are important to their target customer segment. Innovators should test the importance of these factors to their target segment and the customer's satisfaction with currently available solutions. Any gap with the desired customer experience offers an opportunity to shift the market and take over the leadership position.

Let us now understand the core definition of each factor and see how different companies have differentiated themselves to win a major market share.

Requirements

Back in 2005, many companies were trying to differentiate themselves in the crowded cell phone market. Motorola had launched their RAZR line of cellphones, which were good-looking, sleek models targeting a fashion-oriented population who thought of the devices as extensions of their personality. Over a period of four years, Motorola sold about 130 million units[5] of these, a record for flip-style phones.

One company that was successfully serving the business segment was Research In Motion (RIM), with its Blackberry phones. These offered more functionality, allowing users to check emails and track meetings. At that time, these phones were considered "smart phones", as they enabled users to do more than just talk.

Then there was global market leader Nokia, which offered a variety of phones for diverse customer segments. They had the cheapest phone for the low end of the market, as well as a high-end phone for top-tier customers, and a variety of phones in between. They made good-quality phones, and hence became the global market leader.

---

[5] Wikipedia – Motorola RAZR http://en.wikipedia.org/wiki/Motorola_RAZR

There were a host of other players in the industry trying to make their mark and change the overall experience. All these companies were trying to increase their market share by offering incremental features for their cell phones.

On June 11, 1997, Philippe Kahn[6] first demonstrated that pictures could be shared using cell phones. He shared pictures of his newly born daughter Sophie to his relatives using his cell phone; this was the first breakthrough in camera phones, which changed the customer Requirements for the product. Customers rewarded companies offering the ability to take pictures with their phones with a higher market share. The introduction of camera phones changed the Requirements factor of the cell phone experience, and it became one of the differentiating features, until every player in the market offered it. By then, customers wanted more features from their camera phones like better resolution, flash, video, image editing, and sharing features. The cell phone companies kept developing better solutions to meet these Requirements.

As cell phone companies focused on incrementally improving their phone features, one problem area that was not being served well by anyone was the ability to browse the Internet on their phone. This was required to make cell phones the primary device that customers relied on every day, but no one was successful in solving the puzzle until Apple introduced the first iPhone.

Before iPhones, there were companies trying to enable easier internet browsing on a cell phone. They had different ways to allow the customer to browse the internet; they used trackballs, arrow keys and small keyboards to replicate the mouse and keyboard functionality of a personal computer. But all the technologies that worked well on a computer failed on the cell phone, as it was much more difficult to use them when the form factor of the devices

---

[6]Wikipedia – Philippe Kahn http://en.wikipedia.org/wiki/Philippe_Kahn

was so small. Moreover, the keyboard and trackballs took away what very little real estate was available on the cell phone, reducing its screen size. This made it even more difficult to browse the Internet on a phone.

Apple was the first company to use touch technology to solve this challenge. They converted the entire screen into a touchpad and used touch technology for user input. Now customers had bigger screens for browsing, and they were easily able to navigate the Internet, zoom in, and zoom out by just using their fingers.

Using this touch technology, Apple disrupted the Requirements aspect of the customer experience for cell phone customers with the iPhone, which was released on June 29, 2007 and combined the mobility aspects of a regular cell phone with easy-to-use Internet capability. Apple established itself as the "Best-in-Class" provider of the Requirements factor of the customer experience, while every other smartphone manufacturer was shifted down a level. Smartphone customers wanted no fewer features than those provided by Apple's iPhone, and so their current smartphones suddenly did not seem to be meeting their requirements. This differentiation established Apple as a strong new entrant to the cell phone market, and customers rewarded it with significant market share.

By the end of 2007, Nokia was still the leader in the global smartphone market with a 53 percent market share, followed by RIM at 11.4 percent. But though iPhone was launched in the middle of the year and not introduced globally, it captured 6.5 percent of the global smartphone market and about 28 percent of the US market[7], beating Palm and Windows-based smartphones

---

[7] Smart Mobile Device shipment report in 2007 by Canalys.
http://www.canalys.com/newsroom/smart-mobile-device-shipments-hit-118-million-2007-53-2006

within months of its launch. By the end of 2011, Apple was the market leader in the global smartphone market, with a 23.5 percent market share, compared to 12.4 percent for Nokia and 8.2 percent for percent for RIM[8].

Shifting the market by delivering best-in-class experience on the Requirements factor is very powerful, as it awards the innovator who delivers such an experience with significant market share.

But disrupting the Requirements factor of customer experience is the toughest part of innovation. It requires breaking away from the current norm and bringing products or solutions to market that deliver a much better experience than what customers can imagine today. This requires visionary thinking and groundbreaking technologies to provide a better customer experience.

Customer Knowledge Chasm

When Steve Jobs was asked about setting up focus groups by the *Harvard Business Review*, he told them he refused to do so, saying that customers didn't know what they wanted until Apple gave it to them. This echoes Henry Ford, who famously said that if he'd asked people what they wanted, they would have said 'a faster horse'!

These innovative geniuses were specifically looking to disrupt the Requirements factor of the customer experience, which is a challenging problem, as customers really do not know what they want until they see it.

---

[8] IDC Worldwide Mobile Phone Tracker, February 6, 2012
http://www.idc.com/getdoc.jsp?containerId=prUS23299912

While customer feedback is very useful in many cases, it does not necessarily help in disrupting the Requirements factor. This is because even the most visionary and progressive customer cannot imagine how the product could change their day-to-day life. This is what I call the "*Customer Knowledge Chasm*".

For example, before the Nintendo Wii was developed, playing video games was a sedentary exercise, mostly restricted to kids and geeks. No one could imagine that playing a video game would involve moving around as we do in real life, or that it could become a family sport; but Wii changed all that and made playing video games an active enterprise in which every member of the family could participate, enjoy, and even burn some calories.

If Nintendo has asked customers how they would like to play video games, they would have inevitably received responses involving joysticks or game controllers. This is because the majority of customers are not visionary, and current products are their frame of reference; so for them it is very difficult to break away and think of something that is completely disruptive.

Hence the "Customer Knowledge Chasm", as described in Figure 2 .

During the life of a product, the company has many touch points with its customers, most of which help with incremental and sustaining Innovation. Much of the data provided by the customer and the research methodologies are not able to cross the "Customer Knowledge Chasm".

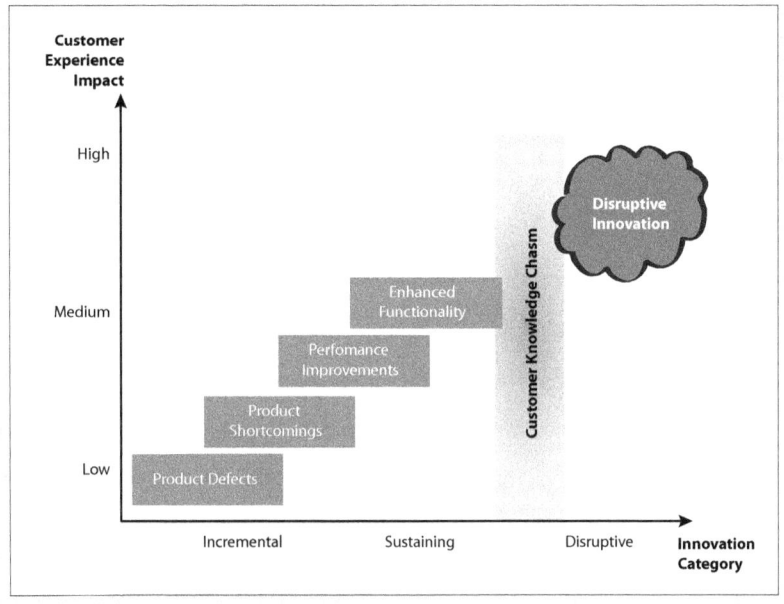

Figure 2: Customer Knowledge Chasm

There are ways to avoid the "Customer Knowledge Chasm", by understanding the job customers are trying to get done, the process that they follow and the ideal outcomes they would like to achieve. By focusing on jobs, process and outcomes, we do not have to rely on the customers' ability to think outside the frame of reference and can avoid the chasm. Innovating to improve the outcomes of the job also ensures that the product is relevant to the customer and something that they would buy.

Price

Consider the example of Southwest Airlines. Once you have booked a ticket with them, you can be sure that there are no additional charges that will be levied. Their famous "bags fly free," "no change fees," and "no additional fees" campaigns were designed to deliver a good Price-focused customer experience. Southwest's claim to fame was that it was an economical airline which sold affordable tickets. Though it is no longer the most Price-competitive airline, it still delivers best-in-class customer experience on this factor. This is because customers know that there are no additional fees to change flights, sit in the exit row or check in two bags. This expectation of no additional fees drives best-in-class Price-focused customer experience. Other airlines cannot make this claim, as they capitalize on every opportunity to charge additional fees; this results in a poor customer experience, particularly to those traveling on a tight budget.

The Price factor of customer experience is not about offering a low-priced product or a high-priced product. It is about managing Price-related customer expectations. A customer looking for the lowest price feels good when she pays less than her expectation, or gets a deep discount. On the other hand, the same customer will feel cheated if she has to pay more than she expected.

Similarly, a customer shopping for expensive articles feels good when the prices are discounted, and is willing to pay more for limited-edition products that are priced higher. For example, If you are in the market for high-end appliances, you are sure to come across Thermador. Their appliances are famous for their innovation, unique and sleek design, value for money, and additional bells and whistles. To deliver a good Price-related customer experience, Thermador controls the street price of their appliances, and does not allow any of its dealers to provide additional discounts. This allows the company to provide a consistent Price-related customer experience, and ensures that its target customers do not feel cheated by a lower-priced Thermador appliance being sold by a rogue dealer.

To be best-in-class for Price-focused customer experience, you need to know your target customer segment's Price expectations and deliver the right experience. If they are looking for low prices, make sure they get the lowest prices and surprise discounts. If they are high-end customers, make sure that the street price is controlled and not discounted.

Availability

You are about to meet an important business client. You plan ahead of time and get to the meeting location early, but you find out that your client is running late. You rehearse your discussion and its key points in your mind a few times, but you still have some time to kill. This is when *Wall Street Journal* app on your iPad comes in handy: you use it to catch up on the various business information, and even get some icebreaker points to share with your client. Having access to this product when you need it delivers a good Availability-related customer experience.

What if the *Wall Street Journal* had never launched this app? You would have had to carry a print copy of the newspaper, in case you had some free time before the meeting. But what if you had forgotten it? In this situation, you do not have access to the *Journal* at a time when you need it the most. This delivers a poor customer experience related to Availability, and creates an opportunity for someone else to exploit the situation by providing a news delivery app for the iPad. If it is from a competitor of the *Wall Street Journal*, it might shift the market to this innovator.

Many companies ignore this factor, but it is one of the key drivers of customer experience. It is driven by the Availability of your product or service when the customer needs it most. Your customers rely on your product or service for their needs, and not being available at a critical time delivers a poor customer experience.

For example, for mobile service providers, this is one of the biggest drivers of customer experience. Many of us have been in situations when we need to make a phone call, but the cellular network is not available. We get frustrated and try to find spots where we can make the call. With data plans, it be even worse, as there are many areas where it is difficult to access the data network. I sometimes use the GPS functionality of my mobile phone for driving directions; once, in downtown Dallas, my mobile phone was unable to access its data network, so it kept guiding me in the wrong direction as it tried to pin down my location. I had stop using my cell phone and revert back to the old-fashioned method of asking for directions.

Similarly, e-commerce websites that do not have the product you are looking for deliver poor customer experience, especially when you are enrolled in paid membership programs. For example, Amazon.com has Prime members who pay an annual membership fee; their expectation is that they will be able to find anything they want to purchase on the Prime network. This helps them avoid any additional fees related to the purchase, including two day shipping, return shipping, or restocking. But there are products that are not available on Amazon.com's Prime network, which drives a poor customer experience as it does not meet the Availability expectations of the customer.

Driving a good Availability-related customer experience is essential for the long-term success of a company, as it ensures that the customer is able to use your product when they need it the most. This is one of the key factors that innovators can use to differentiate against the incumbent and shift the market away from them.

Convenience

Next up is the Convenience factor, which is more complicated than the factors that we have discussed thus far. This is because it needs to deliver different experiences to different customers in different situations. At its core, this factor determines how easy it is for a customer to use your product or service in different situations. So let us look at these situations to understand the Convenience factor.

If you are a retailer, this factor of the customer experience is driven by the time it takes the customer to get to your store, the ease with which he can find the products he wants, and the ease with which he can complete his purchase. For online retailers, getting to the store is not a problem, but how well the customer can get a feel for the product and how fast they can get the product once the order has been placed drives the Convenience factor.

If you are a product company, Convenience is driven by the ease of use of your product. For example, the blood glucose measurement in the late 1970s was cumbersome. Patients had to make an appointment with a laboratory, drive there, provide blood samples, and wait for the results. In the early 1980s, different types of blood glucometers were introduced to enable testing of blood sugar at home. This was still a cumbersome process, however, as it required considerable amounts of blood to be drawn for testing. In addition, it required skill to place the blood drop on the test strip, which led to wastage and inconsistent results. But today, there are blood glucometers that are easy to use; just a small prick gets enough blood for testing, capillary action test strips make sure blood is placed evenly on the strip, and the results are much more accurate. Making this product easy to use increased the market size, as more and more customers bought the glucometer for home use. In 1994, the market was $1.7 billion; but by 2008, worldwide sales climbed to $8.8 billion at an amazing 12.5 percent compound annual growth rate (CAGR)[9].

For a company providing technology to solve business problems, Convenience is driven by ease of customization to fit the client's needs and the ability to use it in day-to-day operations. Consider the example of a widget company planning their manufacturing operations: they get orders to make millions of widgets every month, so it is essential for them to accurately take the orders and manufacture the right quantities. When they were manufacturing these widgets in the hundreds, they used paper to keep track of orders and manufacturing operations. But pretty soon, the process became unreliable, and they started using spreadsheets to track their orders — until one day, when a million-widget order was entered twice by mistake into the spreadsheet. This led to excessive inventory for the company that they could not sell quickly and left them facing a big loss. This is when they decided to implement sales and operations planning software tailored to their business needs. Although the customization of the software took time, it was eventually completed to fit the needs of the manufacturer. Any order that was entered into the sales funnels made its way into the operations planning stack of the software. By analyzing the date of the order, customer code and

---

[9] The Business of Self-Monitoring of Blood Glucose: A Market Profile by Mark D. Hughes, B.S., M.B.A. J Diabetes Sci Technol. 2009 September; 3(5): 1219–1223. Published online 2009 September.

other variables, the software checked for duplicate orders and eliminated them from the operations stack; it also made sure customer commitments were met by scheduling the order at the right time.

So it was that the widget manufacturer found it convenient to have software managing orders and operations, instead of doing it by hand or in a spreadsheet. Not only was the software smart enough to eliminate expensive human errors, but also it delivered a best-in-class customer experience on the Convenience factor to the widget manufacturer.

For all the businesses discussed, best-in-class customer experience on the Convenience factor was delivered by making it easy for the customer to use the product or service. This factor of the customer experience provides the best opportunity for shifting the market, as ease of use encourages more and more customers to use a product, creating a bigger market and a dominant leader.

Service/Support

Post-sale Service/Support is one of the biggest factors of the customer experience in many industries. Companies that deliver poor Service/Support-related customer experience give their customers a reason for taking their business elsewhere, while those who have provided excellent Service/Support earn customer loyalty and repeat business.

Before 1988, for example, most insurance companies were not known for good customer service. Customers paid premiums to these companies, but often found that their Service/Support was not as expected when they needed to make a claim. On November 8, 1988, California voters passed Proposition 103, which forced auto insurance companies to cut premiums by 20 percent and refund premiums to many policyholders. Progressive

was shocked by customer anger, mistrust and dissatisfaction with insurance providers[10]. Companies like Progressive were hit hard by Proposition
103, as more than a quarter of their business was in California. Peter Lewis,
CEO of Progressive, was stunned by its passage, and learned that customers
hated insurance companies for not providing them the required service[11].
This setback changed the fate of Progressive, as it implemented programs to
deliver better Service/Support to their customers.

One newly implemented program was Progressive's "Immediate
Response" claims service, which dispatched an adjuster to policyholders'
homes (and, in many cases, accident sites) as quickly as possible. In case of
emergency, Progressive encouraged its customers to call a toll-free number
which was always answered by a representative 24 hours a day, seven days a
week to take information and authorize emergency measures. A Progressive
claims representative was almost always face-to-face with a customer within
hours of the call.

This level of commitment to Service/Support showed in the financial
results for Progressive Insurance. In 1988 it was the 14th largest insurance
company in America, but by 1995 it had jumped to 4th place. This occurred
even after they had lost a quarter of their business when they pulled out of
California after the passage of Prop 103.

There have been other cases of companies that have differentiated
themselves in a crowded marketplace by delivering best-in-class Service/
Support, including Zappos.com, covered in Chapter 3 of this book.

---

[10] Progressive 1993 10K
[11] Progressive history -
http://www.progressive.com/Progressive-Insurance/AutoBiography/era04_02.swf

Quality

Quality as a customer experience factor has different impacts in different industries. For example, it is one of the most tracked aspects in the auto industry. J.D. Power & Associates publish a yearly index on the quality performance of vehicles released in the United States. The unit of measure is the number of problems experienced over the last 12 months per 100 vehicles (PP100); this measure is published every year for all vehicle brands and for all models, along with an industry average. The vehicles with a lower PP100 are considered to be of high quality.

For a long time, Toyota had low PP100 scores, which made it deliver a good Quality experience. This drove Toyota sales in the U.S., and eventually made it the country's top auto seller. Then it was haunted by quality problems from sticking accelerators, which became one of the leading factors that contributed to its fall to third place.

BMW, on the other hand, had usually performed poorly on PP100. But their full-service maintenance program covers the Quality gap. Under this program, the owner of a BMW does not have to pay for any repairs for 4 years or 48,000 miles; they simply drop their vehicle off at a dealership, drive out in a courtesy vehicle while repairs are being made, and come back to sign a zero-dollar repair bill. This service has driven the Quality factor of customer experience to "Best-in-Class" for BMW, as it is perceived as a low-maintenance, no-headache vehicle.

Toyota focuses on delivering lower PP100 scores, while BMW manages customer perception through its full-service maintenance program. In both cases, they deliver a best-in-class Quality-related customer experience even though they choose different methods.

Every industry has its own Quality measures, and customers expect that the product they purchase delivers a good Quality-related customer experience.

These days, there are customer reviews available online for most products. Online stores like Amazon.com have customer reviews of their products, which helps buyers learn more about product quality and buy only products that deliver a good Quality-related customer experience.

If you are a services company, there are service-related reviews on websites like Yelp.com. These sites let customers write reviews about local service providers and rate their services on a hierarchical scale. These sites make it worthwhile for service providers to focus on Quality as they become an advertisement vehicle for the service provided.

For both product companies and service providers, Quality is a key factor of the customer experience. It is hard to retain a customer when a poor customer experience is provided through this factor, which creates an opportunity for an innovator to shift the market in their favor.

Fashion

During the third quarter of 2004, Motorola released an amazing device that changed the way cell phones were viewed by the customer. Until that time, cell phones were utilitarian objects, often bulky and ugly and never with much character. Motorola launched its first version of the Moto RAZR series, which had a striking appearance and thin profile, making it the most fashionable phone on the market. It was initially marketed as a phone for Fashion-conscious customers, but soon it was available to all market segments and became a great success. After celebrities were seen with this cool-looking phone, excitement was created in the wider market and made the RAZR an immediate best-seller once it was launched to all customer segments.

In 2005, the RAZR became the top-selling cell phone because of its slick features and distinct look. Over the next four years, Motorola sold 130 million RAZR phones and took back market share from Samsung, achieving the second-highest market share position.

The reason for RAZR's success was that it was different; it was compact, stylish and fashionable, so it appealed to a trendier demographic — a younger generation that wanted their cell phone to reflect their personality. The RAZR made the cell phone "cool", and owning one meant that you were part of the in crowd. Feature-wise, the RAZR was not superior to any other cell phone; however, the design made it distinct from anything else available on the market. This helped Motorola regain it #2 position in the market place which it had lost to Samsung not too long ago.

Fashion is not only about the look and feel of a product, but also about the functionality it delivers. To illustrate, let's look at the semiconductor industry. AMD and Nvidia both make graphic processors, which are responsible for delivering high-quality computer graphics. If you are a hardcore gamer, your gaming experience depends on the quality of your graphics processors, as they make the game 'real' for you; so these two companies constantly try to out-innovate each other to deliver a better experience to users. Gamers decide which graphic processor to use based on how realistic the game looks, so although the processors are deeply embedded inside the computer, the ones that provide the coolest graphic experience deliver a best-in-class customer experience in the Fashion factor. The factor is not just about the look and feel of a product, but how "cool" the experience of using it.

The Fashion factor of customer experience is not applicable to all products.

If your product is in a market where people care less about Fashion, like the pharmaceutical industry, you may not need to worry about delivering this experience. But for those markets where the looks or features of a product are important, you should look into a delivering best-in-class customer experience.

Social Responsibility

This factor of the customer experience deals with practices involving social good, and companies following those practices are well-rewarded by customers. A socially responsible company that employs the right practices in the minds of its customer base delivers a good customer experience.

Social good arises from many issues: environmental, religious, commnity-oriented, medical labor practices, to name a few. Whatever the issue, if it appeals to the emotional needs of the customer, it will make an impact on their purchase decisions.

For example, one of the biggest social issues we face today is the abuse of chronic pain relievers (known as opioids, which include morphine and its synthetic variations), which has increased drastically in recent years. In 2006, 5.2 million people surveyed had used pain relievers illicitly — 17 times more than had used heroin[12]. In 2009, over a million emergency room visits were due to abuse of prescription pharmaceuticals[13]. Pharmaceutical drug abusers acquire opioids illicitly and get high by altering the dosage, by crushing, chewing, injecting, inhaling, or taking excessive doses orally.

---

[12] http://emedicine.medscape.com/article/287790-overview#a0199

[13] Drug Abuse Warning Network (DAWN), 2009: National estimates of drug related Emergency Department visits.
http://www.samhsa.gov/data/2k11/DAWN/2k9DAWNED/PDF/DAWN2k9ED.pdf

The Food and Drug Administration's social responsibility is to deliver safe drugs that cannot be abused by the general population. To deliver this Social Responsibility customer experience, the FDA has asked the manufacturers of chronic pain reliever drugs to think of ways to minimize abuse. They have promised priority review of any innovation that can reduce such abuse. One such innovation involves coating the opioid with another substance that reduces its effect or delivers unpleasant side effects to users who try to alter the dosage. For the prescribed user of this drug, there is no change in the effects delivered by it.

Abuse of other drugs, like decongestants and cough suppressants, was also on the rise and forced the FDA to put strict controls on the sale of these medications. Abusers purchase them in large quantities from drugstores and extract high-purity methamphetamine. To put a stop to this abuse, the FDA now requires valid identification from the buyer of these medications. Such controls help the FDA prevent abuse.

The social issue of drug abuse has provided opportunities for pharmaceutical companies to innovate and differentiate themselves in the industry, while enjoying FDA support through faster reviews of their drug filings.

A Social Responsibility customer experience can be delivered by any company, not just those in the pharmaceutical industry. Consider the example of an innovation to reduce the environmental impact of the carpet manufacturing industry: traditionally, carpet is made using petroleum-based raw materials, and has a serious impact on the environment. To start with, it takes a large amount of energy, with sizeable wastage, to manufacture carpets and transport them to installation locations. Carpets have a useful life of 7 to 10 years, after which they are typically dumped into landfills. Since they are not decomposable, they end up harming our environment forever. According to the Carpet America Recovery Effort (CARE), about 3.4 billion pounds of carpets were discarded to landfills in 2010.

Overall, carpet manufacturing, transportation, and disposal have a long-term, irreversible impact on the environment, and there seemed to be no way out of this deadly cycle. But in 1994, Interface Inc. CEO Ray Anderson decided to change this and build an environmentally sustainable carpet company. He set a Mission Zero goal for the company: by 2020, it would have zero impact on the environment. He challenged his employees to innovate every aspect of carpet manufacturing, installation and recycling so that the environmental impact of the company would be reduced without compromising profits. This led to amazing innovations that revolutionized the carpet manufacturing industry.

Interface Inc.'s revenue grew from $800 million in 1995 to $1 billion in 1996, while overall raw material usage dropped by 20 percent[14]. By 2010, it had the following positive impacts on the environment and its operations[15] :

- Energy use per unit was down by 43 percent, which had a clear bottom line impact.
- Eight of nine manufacturing facilities used 100-percent renewable electricity.
- Greenhouse gas emissions were reduced by 44 percent.
- Waste sent to landfills was reduced by 77 percent — about 100,000 tons of material.

---

[14] FastCompany article: Sustainable Growth – Interface Inc. By Charles Fishman published March 31, 1998
[15] Mount Sustainability; Mission Zero Milestones Report :
http://www.interfaceglobal.com/ZazzSustainabilityAssetts/pdfs/Interface_pdf_summary_report.pdf

- A waste reduction program eliminated $433 million in costs since 1995.
- 36 percent of raw materials used are recyclable or bio-based.

Ray Anderson's vision delivered a good Social Responsibility-related customer experience to environmentally-oriented customers, as well as sustainability-oriented growth for Interface Inc.

This is how the Social Responsibility factor of the customer experience can satisfy the customers' emotional needs on environmental issues, religious practices, local community contributions, medical commitments and fair employment practices.

Brand

There are many solutions available for solving a same-customer pain point, and more and more solutions come into the market targeting the same customers. So how to pick the right solution?

This is where the Brand of the company plays a role, as it helps the customer build trust in the company and increases their comfort level for doing business with that company. This factor carries the fruits of good customer experiences and the burdens of bad customer experiences across the other eight factors.

In today's connected world, it is very easy to share both good and bad customer experience stories and reviews with a larger population, and this has an impact on the Brand — and on sales. For example, if your iPhone app is one of many available for solving a customer's pain point, then its customer rating, which reflects the usefulness of your app, has an immense impact on the number of downloads. Unscientific analysis has shown that an app with a 4- or 5-star rating is ten times more likely to be downloaded than an app with a 1- or 2-star rating. This statistic is skewed by many other factors, like Price (free apps get downloaded more) and availability of good competing apps; but, nevertheless, there is a strong correlation between the rating of an app and its number of downloads. Good ratings build Brand awareness, as it helps the app to appear higher up in search results. This can also result in the app receiving wider media coverage, creating much more awareness.

Do not think that ratings are relevant only to the Apple world. There are numerous examples outside the realm of iTunes and the App Store, where ratings help Brand recognition, which in turn helps drives sales for the company.

It is not just good ratings, but bad reviews that go viral in today's hyper-connected world, and that could potentially hurt your Brand. On one occasion, a man with Parkinson's disease was trying to board an Alaska Airlines flight when airline staff, not knowing of his disability, assumed he was drunk and prevented him from catching his flight. Another passenger, witnessing the incident, posted his disgusted reaction on Facebook, complaining about the airline's lack of compassion. The post went viral, and many people started expressing disappointment with Alaska Airline; soon, it became a national story. Alaska Airlines, to its credit, quickly investigated what had happened, apologized, refunded the man's tickets and gave him another round-trip ticket for future use. They recognized that this incident was detrimentally impacting their Brand and rushed to minimize its impact.

Innovators without Brand value struggle to win customers, who will always doubt the innovator's ability to meet their needs. Customers are often unsure if the Quality of a product is good enough, or whether there will be enough post-sale Service/Support; so they will hesitate to give their business to an unknown innovator. On the other hand, if the customer knows enough about the innovator's Brand through reviews or personal references, they are much more likely to do business with them.

In B2B situations, Brand value plays an even bigger role, as companies like to do business with partners they trust. For consumer-focused B2C companies, the Brand aspect of the customer experience is associated with the company itself; but for business-focused B2B companies, the experience is a function of individual relationships within the company Brand. There is a famous saying in the business world: "No one ever got fired for buying IBM equipment". This is the Brand value of IBM. But this alone is not enough for IBM to sell services or products; they have an army of sales personnel who invest time and money in building relationships with the customer. This personal relationship establishes trust between IBM and its customers, and further strengthens its Brand value.

In both B2C and B2B scenarios, Brand is essential to establish the trust to complete the sale.

Customer Experience-Driven Innovation

Now that we have discussed the nine factors of customer experience, let us understand how innovative companies can win by focusing on them.

Innovative companies need to know which customer segments they are targeting, understand their needs, discover gaps in the customer experience, and deliver a "best-in-class" customer experience to cover those gaps. Only then can they establish themselves as a viable option and win new business.

Companies that focus on just one of these nine factors seldom get noticed. Being best-in-class for just one factor does not provide enough incentive for the customer to try your product; customers keep evaluating the company against other options, and are slow in adopting in such cases. Even if the innovators get some early adopters to use and endorse the product, overall market uptake will be small when the innovator delivers a good customer experience across just one factor. Highlight Hunter, the example we discussed in Chapter 1, delivers a best-in-class customer experience for the Convenience factor by making it easy to find highlights in digital videos. But they also need to think about delivering a best-in-class customer experience across two more factors to get more traction from their customer segment.

Delivering best-in-class performance across all nine factors is impractical, as it costs money to be best-in-class for any of the factors, and it might break the bank delivering such a customer experience. Customers will have no problem bringing their business to such a company, and will enjoy the customer experience while it lasts; but this level of customer experience does not generate enough profit for the company to thrive.

A company that delivers a best-in-class customer experience on more than five factors will likely have to change its strategy and ratchet down the customer experience at some point in time. This can lead to negative Brand impact and a poor customer experience. Later in the book you will read about the example of Netflix, which tried to change the customer experience that made them a market leader and experienced negative Brand impact because of it.

To shift the market and win, innovators should ideally focus on 2 – 3 factors that they can positively control and aim to deliver a best-in-class customer experience across these factors. In that way, they are more likely to shift the market away from the incumbent.

This conforms to the "Hedgehog" concept published by Jim Collins in his book *Good to Great*. According to the Hedgehog concept, each organization needs to understand what it can be the best in the world at, and use that understanding to set goals and strategies for the company. Collins also stresses that the company needs to understand what they *cannot* be best at, and not waste their resources or energy on these factors. Companies that follow these principles have gone from good to great.

Depending on the number of resources available, innovators might want to provide a better experience across a few other factors as well. If you are part of a resource-constrained startup, then you should wait until you are able to assess the outcome of your initial strategy. If you are successful, then you will see an uptake in customers using your products. Then you should identify additional one or two factors that are important to your customer segment and match the customer experience delivered by the incumbent. This will ensure that customers who have switched to you (i.e., early adopters) have fewer incentives to switch back to the incumbents, and the customers who are switching to your product find it easier to make a decision. You should keep iterating the customer experience until you have a core set of 5 to 6 factors that are important to your customer segment. Once you get to those factors, you can continue to deliver a better experience and enjoy the shift in the market.

In the next few chapters, we will discuss examples of companies that have successfully shifted the market and emerged as winners in their industry. We will evaluate the customer experiences delivered by these innovators in relation to the incumbents, and see which combination of customer experience factors contributed to the innovators' success. This will help you better understand the framework and its ability to shift markets and to displace incumbents.

Now, let's look at consumer-focused innovation and how innovative companies have toppled the giants and created a place for themselves in crowed marketplaces. This will show you how a combination of factors can help your company deliver a better customer experience and shift the market.

· CHAPTER 3 ·

Consumer-Focused Innovation

Price and Convenience-Focused Innovation

Imagine it is a Friday night in January 1999, and your family decides to spend the night watching a movie. You have two options: either take the family to the nearest movie theater, or rent the latest release from Blockbuster video store.

With five of you in the family, the first option could get pricey, once you weigh up the cost of five tickets, dinner out, and snacks to eat during the movie. If you go to Blockbuster, on the other hand, you'll only spend a few dollars and can enjoy viewing a good movie in the comfort of your own home. So you pick the economical option and decide to rent.

You go to the nearest Blockbuster and search through the aisles for your top three choices. It looks like many people in your area had the same idea, as all available copies of your top two choices have been rented out. So you bag a copy of your third choice and head for the checkout.

Friday nights at Blockbuster tend to be pretty busy, and the time you spend standing in the checkout line feels like eternity. Eventually it's your turn to check out, and you are reminded that this is a one-day rental and you need to return the VHS the next day before midnight, which you don't consider to be a problem. Although the store is only a 10-minute drive from your home, the entire trip takes about 45 minutes. Your spouse is disappointed that you did not get the top two movie choices, but nonetheless the entire family is happy to watch a movie together.

If you think about your experience with Blockbuster up until this point, it would be just fine. This is because you chose them as an economical option, and they lived up to that expectation. Although you did not get the movie you wanted and stood in a long line, you weren't unhappy with the overall experience.

The next day is a big family outing, and you get back home late at night, tired from a long and expensive trip. You are glad that you made it back home just in time before it starts snowing. The entire family is ready to go to bed — and that is when you remember that you have to return the movie to Blockbuster. If you do not return it before midnight you will be charged an extra day's worth of late fees, doubling the cost of the movie. Given the bad snowstorm, you decide to stay home and trust that Blockbuster won't charge the late fee because of the bad weather conditions.

Unfortunately, that's not what happens. You try to explain the situation to a Blockbuster employee, who simply points out that company policy is to charge the late fee no matter what the reason. You are not happy as you pay them the extra money, and swear you will never rent from Blockbuster again. You are not alone.

In 1999, Blockbuster made close to $5 billion renting out movies and video games in the United States and internationally, about $693 million of which was from late fees. They represented 18 percent of Blockbuster's overall rental revenues. Even based on the simple assumption that a customer paid the late fee just once in a year, that means 18 percent of Blockbuster's customers had this poor customer experience. That would make for a lot of unhappy customers — customers who are very likely to jump ship when the next disruptive innovator comes on the scene. This is exactly what happened when Netflix entered the market.

The case of Blockbuster and Netflix is a good example of how an innovative company took advantage of poor customer experience delivered by the incumbent and disrupted the entire market. So how did the customer experience between the two companies compare? And how might that comparison have contributed to Netflix's success?

The target customer segment for Blockbuster was price-sensitive, typically larger families who preferred watching movies in the comfort of their homes. They would instantly recognize Blockbuster stores (Brand) and trusted the stores with personal information like their address, home phone number, and credit card information. This was because Blockbuster was a well-known company and delivered best-in-class Brand-related customer experience. The customer experience delivered by Blockbuster is shown in Figure 3.

Blockbuster had a number of stores at locations convenient to its target customers. They had around 7,700 stores across the United States and in 25 other countries, with most close to home for many of its target population. In fact, Blockbuster claimed in its 2000 annual report that 70 percent of the U.S. population was within a ten-minute drive of one of its stores. Close proximity to the customer made it very convenient to rent a movie from Blockbuster, delivering a best-in-class customer experience on the Convenience factor.

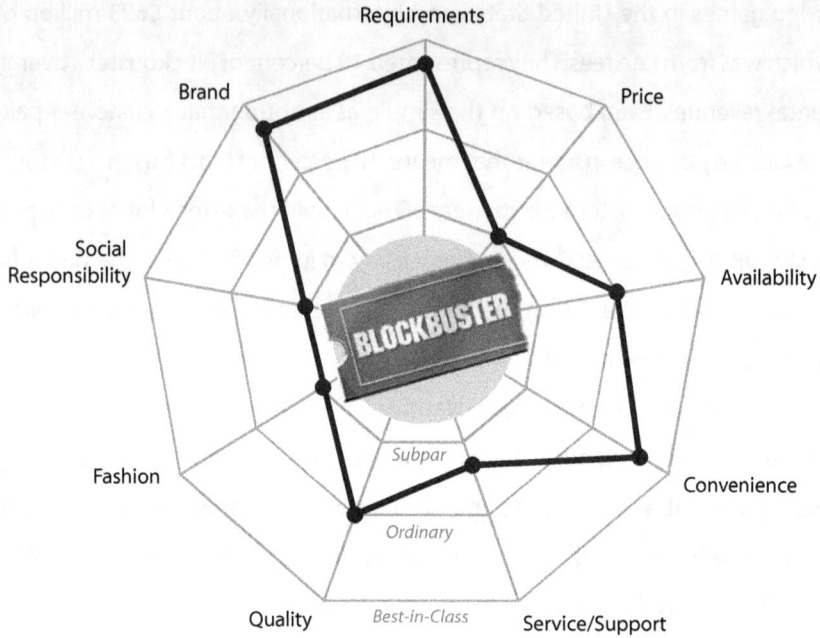

Figure 3: Customer Experience Delivered by Blockbuster

Though it enforced strict rental policies which made customers return the movie on time, come rain or shine. The impact of these strict policies were not as harmful, as there were no better options present at that time.

Blockbuster also had a good reputation for satisfying the need for copies of the latest DVD/VHS movies. They understood the local markets and the needs of the local customer, and they stocked their stores with the right type of movies that appealed to the local population. This ensured that customers found movies interesting to them at their local Blockbuster store, delivering a best-in-class customer experience on the Requirements factor.

Renting movies from Blockbuster was economical when compared to other alternatives, such as watching a movie in a theater. But due to the late fee structure, Blockbuster delivered a subpar Price-related customer experience, as the customer might end up paying much more than expected for the rental — almost double, in many cases. And a customer only needed to pay unexpected late fees once to start feeling bad about doing business with them.

The customer experience on the Availability factor was ordinary due to the fact that customers often weren't able to get their first choice of movie because the store had run out of copies. In addition, it wasn't always possible to find older or less popular titles. In fact, this was one of the advantages that smaller, niche video rental stores had over this branded giant.

By reminding customers to rewind video tapes before returning them, and regularly removing damaged tapes and DVDs, Blockbuster met the Quality expectations of its customers, and rated as ordinary on this factor. However, long lines during peak rental times and staff that did little to help the customer delivered a subpar customer experience on the Service/ Support factor.

Though Blockbuster delivered best-in-class performance on three customer experience factors and ordinary performance on two more, it did deliver poor customer experience to quite a few customers in its target segment. This is because it delivered a subpar customer experience on a factor that mattered the most to this price-sensitive segment: Price! So why did people continue to rent from the store? Why did the customers help Blockbuster grow its revenues, profits, number of stores and even revenues from late fees year over year?

The answer is that most rental chain stores were going bankrupt, and local mom-and-pop stores found it difficult to compete against Blockbuster. It thus became the only option available to most price-sensitive customers, who did not want to spend money watching movies in the theater.

This was the case until one day Reed Hastings, founder and CEO of Netflix, was charged late fees for returning his movie late. This inspired him to start his own movie rental business along with a few colleagues.

Netflix started off by disrupting the Convenience factor of the Blockbuster customer experience. They took the internet and combined it with the U.S. Postal Service to deliver movies right to customers' doorsteps. Suddenly, the local Blockbuster store 10 minutes away was not that convenient for customers, and so the Convenience factor of the customer experience delivered by Blockbuster fell from best-in-class to ordinary levels. Moreover, customers did not have to search through aisles of titles in Blockbuster stores to find the movie they wanted to rent; they could find it online at Netflix.com by using its search function. So Netflix became a more convenient option for renting movies.

But there was still a problem: Netflix had a similar late fee policy as Blockbuster, and also charged shipping and handling fees for mailing the rental. So Netflix was not a great option for the price-sensitive customer segment. There were customers who were willing to pay the additional fees for the convenience of having movies delivered to their homes, but this segment was small. For the price-sensitive customer segment, Blockbuster still continued to be the better option.

Netflix tried lowering its prices and extending its rental periods, but was able to rent only 250,000 discs in the first year of its operations[16]. It quickly learned that Convenience alone would not get them the required attention, and they need to deliver a better customer experience on additional factors.

---

[16] Business 2.0 Magazine: "How Netflix is fixing Hollywood" By Christopher Null, July 1 2003;
http://money.cnn.com/magazines/business2/business2_archive/2003/07/01/345263/index.htm

After a few starts and stops, Netflix decided to distinguish itself from Blockbuster on the key factor that mattered the most to the price-sensitive customer segment: Price.

In September 1999, Netflix launched a monthly subscription model with unlimited rentals, no late fees and no shipping & handling fees. For a flat fee of $19.95 per month, customers could rent up to three DVDs at a time. It was the all-you-can-eat buffet of DVD rentals, and customers could watch as many movies as they wanted for one flat price.

This, combined with the Convenience factor of having the DVDs delivered to customers' doorsteps, delivered a much better customer experience to the price-sensitive segment. Customers were able to better budget for movie rentals, as the monthly subscription price did not vary by the number of titles that were rented or the length of time the customer held on to the movie. With this flat-fee rental model, Netflix delivered a best-in-class customer experience related to Price and clearly differentiated itself from Blockbuster.

A side-by-side comparison of the customer experience delivered by both Blockbuster and Netflix in the year 2000 is shown in Figure 4.

Since Netflix was an online business with no stores, it could theoretically offer a huge number of titles on its website. Blockbuster store carried about 1,500 titles, while Netflix carried around 12,000[17]. In this way, Netflix more than met Blockbuster on the Requirements aspect of customer experience.

Netflix also built a recommendation engine that would suggest a movie to its subscribers based on their ratings of various movies in its catalog. This, combined with the search engine for finding movies, made it convenient for a subscriber to find the right rental.

---

[17] Strategy by John Ellis at FastCompany.com published on October 31, 2002; http://www.fastcompany.com/magazine/64/jellis.html

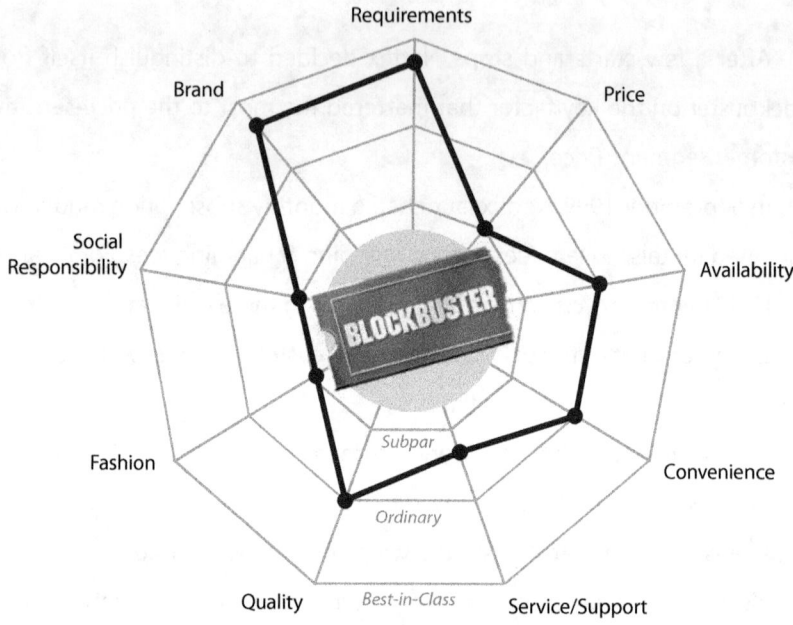

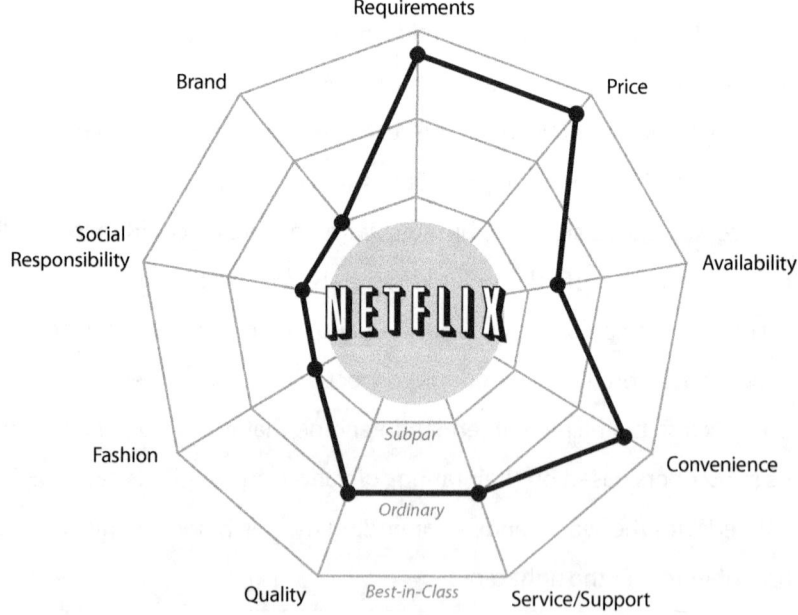

**Figure 4: Comparison of Customer Experiences Delivered by
Blockbuster and Netflix in the Year 2000**

So Netflix delivered a best-in-class customer experience across Price and Convenience factors, and differentiated itself from Blockbuster. This created a strategic advantage for Netflix and gave customers a reason to try out its services; but it was still a long way from becoming the market leader.

There were some aspects of Netflix's customer experience that were not that great. The rental limit of three DVDs at a time created some availability concerns; for example, you could end up having no movies to watch on a Friday night, because you forgot to mail back the three DVDs that were with you for more than a week. Also, it took anywhere from three to five days for a DVD to reach most parts of the country from Netflix's distribution centers, so customers had to plan well ahead of time if they had to watch a recent movie on a Friday night. I had a few friends who were very smart about this and developed a circulation mechanism: they made sure that they had one DVD in transit *from* Netflix, one to watch at home, and one in transit back *to* Netflix. But not all customers were as smart; for many, their ability to watch a movie on Friday night depended on the planning they did the week before. For these reasons, Netflix delivered a subpar customer experience on the Availability factor.

Just like Blockbuster, Netflix met customer requirements and delivered good quality product, but it did not have good Brand value compared to Blockbuster.

In the early 2000s, Netflix delivered a best-in-class customer experience on three factors, compared to only two for Blockbuster. Netflix's subscription price was better than Blockbuster's rental fee plus late fee. Since the DVDs were delivered to the home and were easy to find on Netflix's website, it delivered better customer experience in Convenience. These were the two factors that price-sensitive and convenience-seeking customers cared about, and Netflix made sure that it was best-in-class across these factors.

After a period of time, Netflix began not only to offer most titles available from Blockbuster, but also gained the ability to offer titles which were not to be found in any Blockbuster stores. Because of this, Netflix was able to beat Blockbuster on the Requirements factor of customer experience.

Better performance on these three factors of customer experience enabled Netflix to win more and more of Blockbuster's customers and become a promising challenger to the movie rental industry giant.

At the end of the year 2000, Netflix had 292,000 subscribers and annual revenues of $36 million. This growth in subscribers continued, and Netflix had a successful IPO just two and half years after starting its innovative business model.

To improve the subpar customer experience it delivered to customers on Availability, Netflix used money from its IPO to open 10 more distribution centers across the country. This reduced the shipping times from three to five days to one day for 90 percent of all U.S customers[18]. While this improved the customer experience, when compared to Blockbuster, it was still a subpar customer experience on the Availability factor, as a customer could get a DVD from Blockbuster within an hour. Customers did not seem to care much for this aspect of customer experience, however, as they gave more and more business to Netflix. Netflix doubled its number of subscribers every year, and the end of 2004, it had 2.6 million subscribers and an annual revenue of $500 million.

Netflix was very successful with their online rental business model, which attracted competitors like Walmart and, naturally, Blockbuster to the market

---

[18] Strategy by John Ellis at FastCompany.com published on October 31, 2002; http://www.fastcompany.com/magazine/64/jellis.html

to offer their own online subscription services. This led to price wars in the industry, which were eventually won by Netflix due to the volume of its subscribers. Both Blockbuster and Walmart's services were not profitable and were eventually shut down.

By the end of 2004, Blockbuster recognized the poor customer experience it was delivering, and in December 2004 it announced the end of late fees. But by then it had allowed a fierce competitor into the industry that had a successful IPO and was on a path to growth. At its peak in 2004, Blockbuster had 9,100 stores, but in an effort to return to profitability, it started closing stores. It had many opportunities to improve its customer experience and even an opportunity to acquire Netflix, but it did not pursue any of them.

By 2010, Blockbuster was down to 6,500 stores, and had reintroduced late fees to increase its revenues. Fewer stores meant that customers had to drive longer distances to reach one, and hence it was no longer convenient to rent from Blockbuster. Late fees, of course, were never appreciated by the price-sensitive customer segment; but unlike in 1999, customers had other alternatives and they did not have a reason to rent from Blockbuster. The company kept losing money every year, and eleven years after Netflix launched its flat fee subscription model with no late fees, Blockbuster filed for bankruptcy.

This example demonstrates how innovative companies that deliver a better customer experience to their target customer segment win and displace the industry incumbents. It does not matter how big the incumbent is, or how much control it has over the market; innovative companies will win if they become best-in-class at delivering a customer experience that matters to the target customer segment.

Once Blockbuster declared bankruptcy, the price wars were over and Netflix emerged as a clear market leader. By this time, Netflix had established a good reputation (Brand) as a company that makes it easy to rent DVDs and to stream videos over the internet (Convenience) at an affordable flat fee per month (Price). It had a wide selection of good DVDs and Blu-Ray discs, and many titles available for online streaming (Requirements). Through over 50 distribution centers, it ensured that most of the U.S. population got DVDs with a one-day turnaround time, and its online streaming model ensured that customers could watch movies on demand (Availability). They made sure that the DVDs were in good condition (Quality) before shipping them off to customers, and that their staff was available to answer any concerns (Service/Support). The customer experience delivered by Netflix in 2011 is shown in Figure 5.

By 2011, Netflix delivered a best-in-class customer experience across five factors and ordinary customer experience across two additional factors. This created a great deal of financial pressure on the company, and was not sustainable over the long run.

To understand this further, let us analyze Netflix's financial statements. In 2009's 10K filings, we can see that the subscriber base grew by 30 percent to 12 million and the corresponding revenue growth was 22 percent. But to support the high levels of customer experience, headcount for shipping and customer service centers increased by 14 percent. The financials in 2010 were more challenging, as the subscriber base grew by 63 percent to 20 million, but revenues only increased by about 30 percent and headcount by 10 percent. The average revenue per paying subscriber was $13.30 in 2009, and declined by 8 percent to $12.19 in 2010.

So it was clear to Netflix that every new subscriber was bringing in less average revenue, but continued to contribute to the increase in head-count expenses. The company wanted to increase revenues by increasing

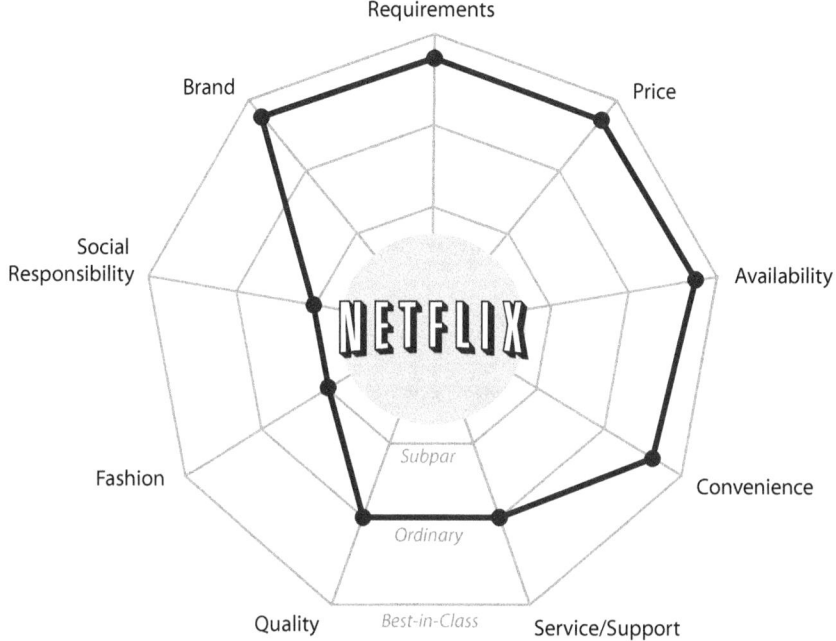

Figure 5: Netflix Customer Experience in 2011

the average revenue per subscriber. Since its biggest competitor was no longer strong, Netflix decided to move away from price war-era pricing. It announced a 60 percent increase in monthly subscription costs for its customers, unbundled the rental and online streaming businesses, and tried to separate the businesses into Netflix and Qwikster.

The problem with this strategy was that Netflix was trying to redefine the customer experience that was the sole reason for its success in the industry. Had it gone ahead with its plan, Netflix would have gone down on the Price, Availability and Convenience factors of customer experience. Customers were used to paying the low monthly subscription fees, and the increase in Price was at odds with the customer experience that they had come to expect. Also, having two separate accounts for DVD rentals and online streaming without any data and information sharing between the two was not Convenient, as a customer would have to log in to different sites for managing their video list. It would also impact Availability because online streaming did not have as many titles, and DVDs are not be available for watching on demand due to postal delays.

By cutting down on these three factors of customer experience, Netflix hoped to a make higher average revenue per customer and cut down its related expenses, but the customer backlash made it reverse some of its plans. It still went ahead with a price increase of about 60 percent and separate pricing for its online streaming and DVD services, which resulted in increase in customer cancellations during the third quarter of 2011. Netflix's churn, which measures average customer cancellations in a month, increased to 4.9 percent in 2011 from 3.8 percent in 2010. The unique domestic net new additions to the subscriber base for 2011 decreased by 32.3 percent when compared to 2010. Customers who had the bundled online streaming and DVD packages cancelled their subscriptions or moved to the less expensive online streaming service alone. In fact, 73.6 percent of new subscribers chose only the unlimited streaming plan, priced at $7.99, which resulted in a further 8.3 percent decrease in average revenue per paying customer to $11.84 in 2011 from $12.20 in 2010. Overall DVD mailing expenses declined by 13.7 percent, but total number of hours of streaming content viewed increased.

This change in Netflix's financial performance points to the fact that the customer segment Netflix is serving is price-sensitive and convenience-focused. When forced by Netflix to choose a plan, they chose the less expensive unlimited streaming plan that let them view content on demand, even though there were significantly less titles available for online streaming compared to DVD rentals. Overall, Netflix's revenues and subscriber base grew in 2011, but was skewed towards a plan that provided the desired customer experience to its target segment — the $7.99 unlimited streaming plan. This clearly shows that customers expect a certain customer experience from Netflix, and do not want to change their expectations. So when given an option, they would choose the option that delivers the same customer experience.

Did customers stop renting DVDs? Where did they watch the latest movies that were not available for online streaming from Netflix? Fortunately for these customers, there was another retail option that was growing aggressively and offering good-quality DVD rentals at cheaper rates and at convenient locations.

The movie rental industry story would be incomplete without mentioning the biggest challenger in the industry: Redbox. Back in 2002, McDonald's experimented with 11 fully automated Redbox DVD rental kiosks at its restaurants; the experiment was successful, leading to a full-market rollout of these kiosks in Denver, Colorado in 2004. Since then, Redbox has been growing aggressively, opening more kiosks and gaining market share of physical DVD rentals. Its DVD rental model is similar to that of Blockbuster, but much more convenient and less expensive.

Redbox was initially owned by McDonald's, so it installed kiosks only in its restaurants. But in 2005, Coinstar invested in Redbox, making it an independent company. This opened numerous opportunities for Redbox, which started deploying kiosks at grocery stores, convenience stores, drug stores, gas stations and mass merchant locations. From 2005 to 2009 it added some 18,000 kiosks across the country before Coinstar bought the remaining shares of the company, making it a wholly owned subsidiary[19].

According to Coinstar's 2011 financial statements, Redbox has 35,400 kiosks in 29,300 locations across the United States[20]. About 85 percent of Coinstar's $1.85 billion revenue in 2011 was from Redbox. Though the DVD rental market did not do well in 2011 and decreased by 11 percent, Redbox rentals seemed unaffected by this market dynamic, as its rentals increased by 28 percent[21]. Ironically, right around the time Netflix announced significant price increases, Redbox claimed that 68 percent of the U.S. population lived within a five-minute drive from one of its kiosks. In March 2012, it crossed the two-billion rental milestone, with a 37 percent market share of disc rentals in the United States.

The customer experience delivered by Redbox is shown in Figure 6. The success that Redbox has had over the last decade clearly shows the value it brings to a customer segment that was not being served well by Blockbuster or Netflix. This is a price-sensitive segment that cannot justify a fixed monthly subscription, as they might not rent movies regularly. For example, a customer who only watches movies on Friday nights would watch 4 to 5 movies a month. Renting these movies at Redbox would cost anywhere from $4.80 to $6, depending on the movie, which is much less than a monthly subscription at Netflix. But if a customer rents more than five movies a month, Netflix might be a better option. Redbox rental prices are less than those of Blockbuster as well; hence, it delivers best-in-class customer experience on Price.

---

[19] Redbox Timeline: http://www.redbox.com/image/mediacenter/timeline-3-8-12b
[20] Redbox 2011 10K:
[21] Thinking outside the Redbox by Nick Wingfield in New York Times; Published February 17, 2012

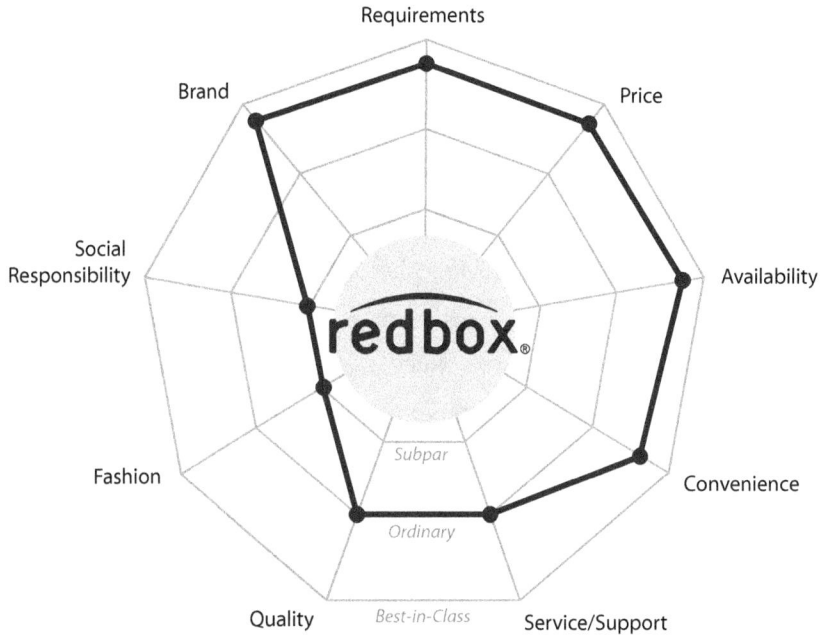

Figure 6: Redbox Customer Experience

It is convenient to get the DVDs shipped to the home, but it is equally convenient to rent out movies when customers are doing their errands, grocery shopping or filling up on gas at a 7-Eleven store. Moreover, the kiosks are easy to use, movies available in the kiosk are easy to find, customers can reserve a movie to be picked up at a particular kiosk, and it is easy to rent. All of these ease-of-use features, along with the convenient locations, help Redbox deliver a best-in-class customer experience on Convenience.

The vast majority of Redbox kiosks are located in customer-trusted branded stores like CVS, Walmart and Walgreens. This presence has improved the company's perceived Brand value, which helped it gain trust and attract even more customers. It therefore delivers a best-in-class customer experience on Brand. It has many of the latest movies in DVD and Blu-Ray formats, and claims to have new movies available sooner than they are on Netflix, which makes it deliver a best-in-class customer experience on Requirements.

Availability is not always guaranteed, but customers can go online and reserve a copy of a desired movie to be picked up at a particular kiosk, so Redbox delivers an ordinary experience on Availability. Similarly, there is nothing special about the Quality-related customer experience, as the company tries to keep good-quality disks in circulation. As Redbox is an automated operation with no human interaction, Service/Support is only available online or by phone, but the phone service they provide appears to be good.

Recently, one of my friends reserved a movie online and went to pick it up at the closest CVS pharmacy. When she arrived, she found that the kiosk was not working, so she called the number on the kiosk and was promptly answered by a customer service representative (CSR). He acknowledged that the kiosk had not been working for the past 30 minutes and an engineer was on his way to fix it. The CSR offered a promotional code to cover the charges that were incurred by my friend, and offered to reserve the movie at the next-nearest kiosk. Though the kiosks are fully automated, there are people behind the scenes who are on top of the situation, working to resolve any problems.

Overall, there are customer segments that find it economical and convenient to rent from Redbox. Based on the history of competition and survival rates in this industry, we know that the company that provides the best and most meaningful customer experience to the target segment will win. It is yet to be seen who will survive and thrive in the battle between Netflix and Redbox; perhaps both.

Blockbuster, meanwhile, is still trying to win back its customer base. It recently sent out mailers to its customers offering them a free month of rentals and a 99-cent price point. But it is difficult for customers to go back to a Brand that delivered poor customer experience for years; that Brand now has many negative connotations and delivers a subpar customer experience, making it difficult to for it compete against Netflix or Redbox.

Fashion-Focused Innovation

Now let us look at another example of how a small startup in New York competed against a global incumbent and quickly became successful. In January 2010, Jason Goldberg and Bradford Shellhammer launched Fabulis. com, a social networking website for the gay community; the initial vision of the founders was to become Yelp, Groupon and Facebook for gays and lesbians. Jason Goldberg was a successful serial entrepreneur who had successfully exited a number of ventures, and Bradford Shellhammer was good with design. They launched the website, which managed to attract 110,000 total customers and about 30,000 active users[22]. Though they built a good website, Fabulis.com did not deliver a differentiated customer experience compared to Yelp, Groupon or Facebook, so gay customers did not feel the need to use this website.

By early 2011, the founders realized that they need to do something different, so they shut down the site in order to develop a newer, un-served niche where they could be much more successful — one based on design. In June 2011, they launched Fab.com, a flash sales website (a site that offers

---

[22] Entrepreneur.com article: Fab Forward: How Fab.com Found a Niche in a Design Deal Social Hub by Jason Ankeny published October 18, 2011

products at deep discounts for a limited period of time) for the fashion-oriented customer segment.

When Fab.com decided to move away from the gay market to a flash sales market, they entered an overcrowded marketplace with players like Amazon, branded retail stores/websites, and many other flash sales websites. All these retail outlets offered price discounts and had spent a lot of money to attract customers to their sites/stores. So how could a start-up compete against these seasoned incumbents? Fab.com did so by focusing on delivering a customer experience that was different from any other retailer.

Online and retail shoppers have different expectations based on what they are looking for, and the time of the year. During the holidays, they want a wide choice of gifts at throwaway prices; at times like Valentine's Day they want to find cool surprises; and throughout the year they want to find the items they need at a reasonable price, or with a memorable customer experience. Retailers and websites that have successfully differentiated on the customer experience they deliver have seen repeat customers. In order to understand how Fab.com differentiated itself in the overcrowded retail space, let us compare it with the customer experience delivered by other types of retailers in a variety of shopping situations.

High-end retailers, like Neiman Marcus or Louis Vuitton, attract shoppers who are looking for specific high-end fashion products. Over the years, these high-end retailers have improved their ability to attract and sell to both impulse buyers and fashion-oriented shoppers by delivering a good customer experience. They meet customer requirements by providing them the products they are looking for; hence, their Requirements factor of the customer experience is best-in-class. They make it convenient for the customer to shop in their stores, but the stores are few and far apart, making

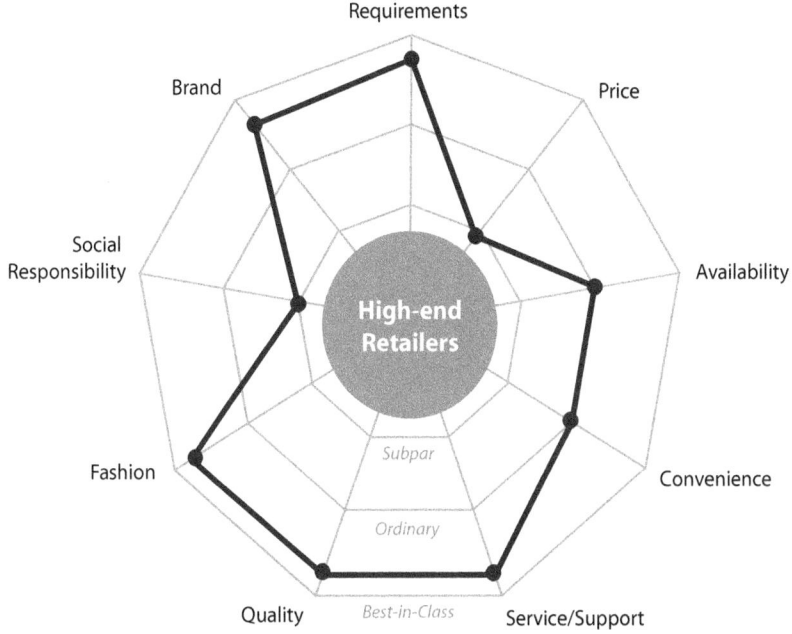

Figure 7: Customer Experience Delivered by High-End Retailers

it inconvenient for shoppers to get to their stores. Thus, their customer experience on Convenience is ordinary.

The prices in these stores vary quite a bit, and when a new set of fashionable products make it to the stores they are not discounted. As time goes by, however, they need to clear the inventory in the store and start offering deep discounts on these products. This drives a not-so-pleasant customer experience for those who bought the same product at full price, so the Price-related customer experience is subpar.

These retailers provide good service, and offer high-quality products that are very fashionable, so they deliver a best-in-class customer experience on Service/Support, Quality and Fashion. They cannot guarantee that the specific item that the customer is shopping for is available in the store, but they can get it shipped to the customer's home through their online stores; hence, they typically deliver an ordinary customer experience on Availability factor. The customer experience delivered by these high-end retailers is shown in Figure 7.

Now let's review the shopping experience delivered by online retailers like Amazon.com. The key to Amazon's success is to deliver a customer experience that makes the customer think of them first when shopping online. They are focused on attracting customers who know what they want, and are looking to buy soon, so they make sure that they have what the customer is looking for, at the right price, in a convenient online location, and with reasonable customer support. They have a variety of items available, such as books, toys, electronics, games, and watches, but the primary factors that they differentiate on are Price, Convenience and Availability. The Price factor is very important for online shopping, and they deliver this by making sure that their prices are highly competitive. Amazon makes it convenient for customers to find the products they want to buy through a very efficient search engine; they also have a good recommendation engine, which suggests products to the customers based on the buying history of other, similar users. These, coupled with free two-day shipping for Prime customers and free regular shipping for all customers on most items, make it convenient to shop at Amazon.com. The customer experience delivered by Amazon.com is shown in Figure 8.

Between the high-end retailers and Amazon, the Fashion, Convenience, Price, Service/Support and Quality factors of the customer experience have already been covered. So how could Fab.com differentiate itself by offering something new to fashion-oriented customers?

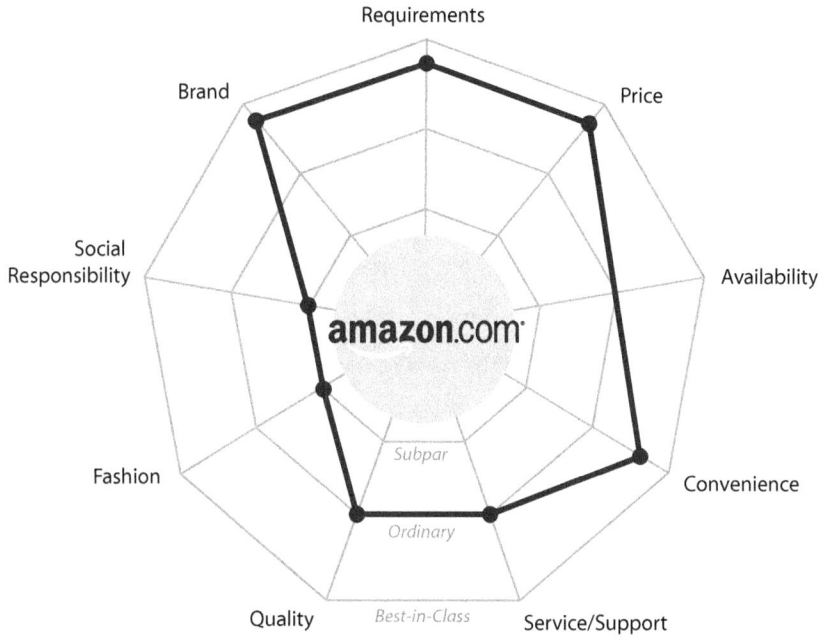

Figure 8: Amazon.com Customer Experience

First and foremost, they achieved this by focusing on design, delivered through an attractive website that offers cool products with high visual appeal to fashion-oriented shoppers. Visitors to Fab.com are not necessarily looking for a specific item; they do, however, want access to some cool, visually appealing products they wouldn't find anywhere else. Every day at Fab.com, customers can find a wide variety of products including artwork, jewelry, and designer furniture with prices ranging from one dollar to more than $1,000. Fab.com does not restrict itself to a core set of designers; rather, it offers any product that has attractive designs that would appeal to its customer base. This kind of variety is difficult to find in high-end retail stores, which is how Fab.com differentiates itself by offering more Fashion-oriented products.

Fab.com also offers deep discounts for a limited time, which tempts customers to make impulse purchases. These discounts include their daily sales of up to 70 percent off, with most prominent discounts in the 25 percent to 45 percent range. These sales are offered for only 72 hours, and shoppers see a counter on top of each product page that creates an urgency to buy. Also, when the customer adds the item to their shopping cart, they have only 15 minutes to make the purchase; after that time, the item is automatically removed from the cart. This also creates a sense of urgency for the customer, and helps the impulse buyer to make a decision.

It is great to offer fashionable products at deep discounts and get impulse buyers to make that purchase, but for a business to be successful and attract enough paying customers, it needs to satisfy the customer experience across at least three factors. This is true for Fab.com as well, as it needs customers to visit its website and trust it enough to share their credit card information. Also, when a website creates a sense of urgency for buying the products it is especially essential for the customer to trust the company. This is where the need for a strong Brand comes in for Fab.com, and the founders did a great job of building the brand with a limited budget.

Before launching the website, Fab.com signed up about 175,000 customers through various viral marketing activities and strategic advertising[23]. This ensured that the suppliers were willing to sell products at Fab.com, as the site now had a decent customer base. Fab.com built a social sharing capability into the website, and encouraged their customers to share their

---

[23] Entrepreneur.com article: Fab Forward: How Fab.com Found a Niche in a Design Deal Social Hub by Jason Ankeny published October 18, 2011

purchase information with friends on social networks like Facebook. Many customers were happy to share the information about the cool products that they bought at Fab.com; this created further brand recognition and attracted more customers to the website.

After getting an initial set of customers and some modest success, the Fab.com founders shared their story of converting a failure into a success through traditional and online social media. This topic is of interest to many people, and after reading about their success story, people started exploring Fab.com. Blogs, news articles, presentations, videos, Twitter feeds, and Facebook shares began buzzing with the Fab.com success story. This created global Brand value for the company, and they saw their customer base increase exponentially. Just over a year after launching the website, Fab.com had 4.5 million users, 2 million orders, over $100 million in run-rate and revenues expected to cross half a billion dollars in 2013[24].

Figure 9 shows the customer experience delivered by Fab.com, which is best-in-class on three factors: Fashion, Brand and Price. It is not a website that customers visit when they want to buy a specific product, as that product might not be available on the website. Fab.com does not store any inventory, and it passes orders on to sellers for fulfillment. This leads to long delays in shipment. Most customers expect an e-commerce website to ship their orders as soon as it is placed, so Fab.com does not meet this particular requirement of the online shopper, and hence delivers a subpar customer experience on the Requirements factor.

---

[24] Techcrunch Article – Fab Seeking to Raise $100M at Super Fab Valuation by Alexia Tsotsis: http://techcrunch.com/2012/05/21/fab-seeking-to-raise-100m-at-a-super-fab-valuation/

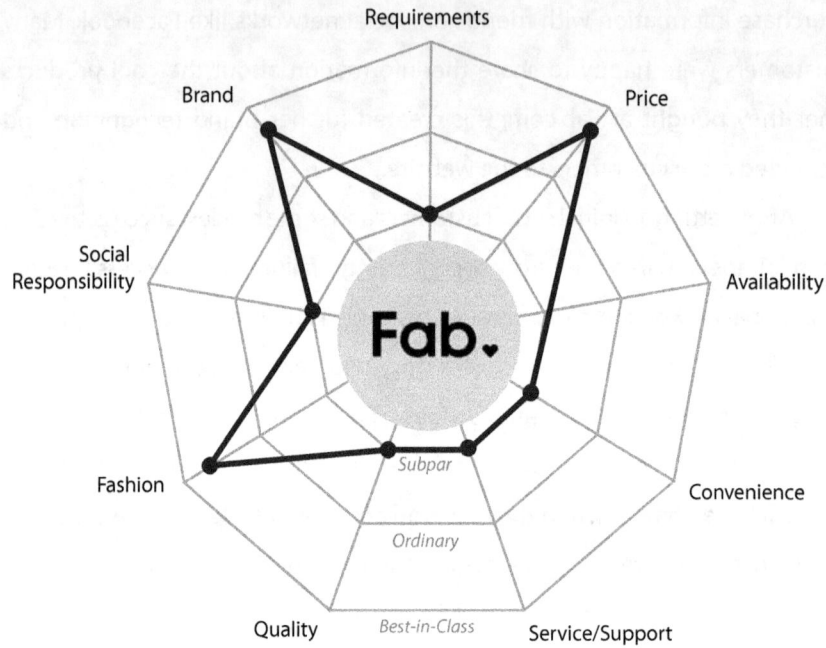

Figure 9: Fab.com Customer Experience

As you can see from Figure 9, Fab.com scores subpar on three factors of the customer experience: Availability, Convenience, and Support/Service. Because the site offers products on sale for only 72 hours, and are available in limited quantities, customers are often disappointed to find that their chosen item is out of stock (Availability). The lack of a search engine on the site makes it challenging for visitors to find specific products, brand names, or designers, thereby detrimentally impacting the Convenience factor. There is a long delay between the time the customer places an order and receives the shipment, there is currently no way to track the status of an order, and the company offers no return policy; all of these factors drive a subpar customer experience on Service/Support. This shows in Fab.com reviews from the shoppers; at the time of this writing, Reviewcenter.com featured 113 reviews on Fab.com with an average Service/Support rating of 2 stars out of 5. Reading the reviews reveals many complaints about Service/Support being unresponsive and non-existent.

Finally, because the products that Fab.com sells are delivered directly from the manufacturers, it has no control over quality or delivery, hence delivering a subpar customer experience on the Quality factor. Referring back to the Reviewcenter.com, there are comments about shipping delays, incorrect shipments, bad packaging, and many other such problems, which might be outside of Fab.com's control but still affects the customer experience it delivers. Overall, Fab.com has an average rating of 1.5 stars, with only about 12.4 percent of Reviewcenter.com users recommending the website.

Nevertheless, Fab.com has experienced good growth and profitability by focusing on the three factors of the customer experience that they do well: Price, Fashion and Brand. To continue growing, though, it will need to offer a better customer experience across a few other factors as well. Just charming customers with good design is not going to help them grow to the next level. Unless Fab.com can boost their level of customer experience across other factors, the Brand is likely to carry the burden of bad customer experiences for a long time.

Fab.com is a great example of how innovative companies can be successful by delivering a good customer experience on just three factors, the minimum number required for achieving customer attention. Similarly, innovative companies looking to differentiate themselves in a crowded marketplace should figure out which three factors can help them differentiate and deliver a good experience.

Service/Support-Focused Innovation

Another e-commerce company that tops the list in customer experience-driven innovation is Zappos.com. The company almost shut down in 1999, but changed their culture and focused on delivering "happiness" to customers. It became best-in-class at delivering service to its customers, and as a result grew to be North America's largest online shoe store.

In 1999, Tony Hsieh invested his own money in the company, and created a culture focused on happiness. His philosophy was that happy employees would deliver happiness to customers. To make this philosophy work, he invested heavily in building the core values and culture of the company. Every employee got five weeks of training on these aspects of the business. Candidates were interviewed more on cultural fit than on previous experience; performance reviews were based on adherence to core values and culture, which helped to reinforce the focus over time.

Tony's philosophy of happiness delivered a good customer experience and helped him differentiate his offering in a crowded shoe retail space. Happy customers led to good financial results for Zappos.com; by the end of 2008, it had more than $1 billion in revenues from close to 10 million customers, 40 percent of whom brought repeat business. In fact, on any given day, about 75 percent of Zappos.com purchases were from repeat customers. In the fourth quarter of 2007, first-time buyers spent an average of $124, while repeat customers spent closer to $156[25]. In November 2009, Zappos.com was purchased by Amazon.com for $1.2 billion.

---

[25] Institute of Business Forecasting, Demand Planning and Forecasting: Best Practices Conference. Amanda Nevins, Chief Accounting Officer and VP Finance, Zappos.com

Now let's review the customer experience delivered by Zappos.com as shown in Figure 10 and how they innovated to deliver that experience.

Zappos.com's tagline, "Powered by Service", clearly communicated the Brand value of the company, and it was strictly followed by all employees. To deliver amazing Service/Support, it offered a 365-day return policy, free overnight shipping, free return shipping and a 24/7 toll-free number to call.

The company's CSRs are not only trained to assist the customer to the best of their abilities; they are even trained to refer a customer to a competitor if they were not able to provide assistance. For example, on one occasion, a customer called late at night to find out which nearby pizza joint was still open, and the CSR not only helped them with that, but went ahead and ordered them the pizza. There are no sales-based performance goals for CSRs at Zappos.com, and no limits on the amount of time they may spend talking to a customer. The only goal is to provide the best shopping experience possible. This makes Zappos.com a best-in-class customer Service/Support company.

Happy customers share their experiences with others, which has led to strong, loyal customer base. Initially, Zappos.com hardly had an advertising budget, but it kept doubling its revenue every year just through word of mouth. This has led to creation of a strong Brand.

To deliver Convenience, Zappos.com carries the inventory of all its products in a warehouse that runs 24/7. In 2003, it stopped drop shipping (where it took orders and relied on the supplier to fulfill them), as it could not rely on its suppliers to deliver the right kind of customer experience.

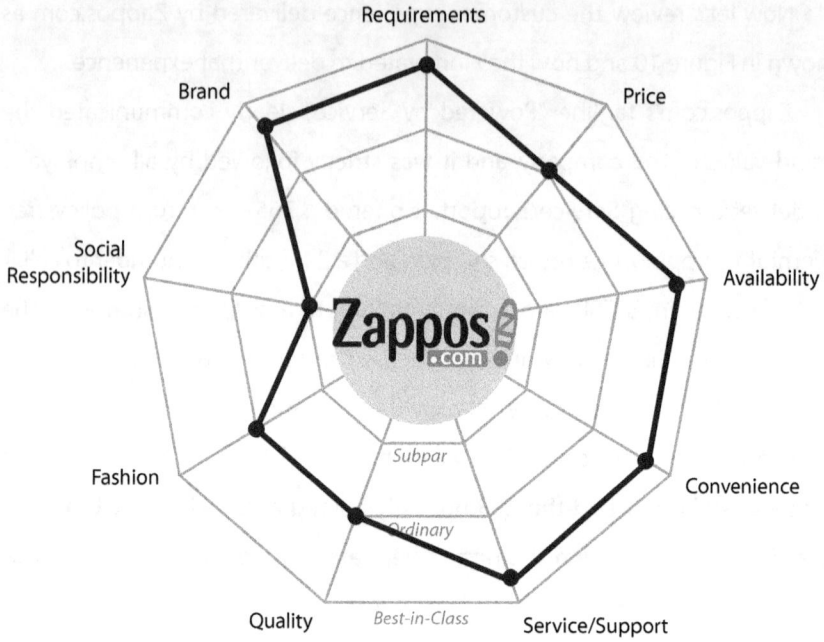

Figure 10: Zappos.com Customer Experience

Zappos.com carries over four million items in its warehouse, consisting of more than 1,200 brands, over 200,000 styles, and close to a million unique SKUs.[26] By having such a large inventory, it makes sure that it meets customer needs (Requirements) and has the right item available (Availability) for shipping at a moment's notice. Managing such a large inventory can be challenging, so Zappos.com assigns a unique license plate to each product that it scans into the system along with its location on the shelf[27]. This helps employees find the exact location of each item ordered in next to no time.

---

[26] Institute of Business Forecasting, Demand Planning and Forecasting: Best Practices Conference. Amanda Nevins, Chief Accounting Officer and VP Finance, Zappos.com

[27] Delivering Happiness: A Path to Profits, Passion, and Purpose by Tony Hsieh

The company also takes high-quality photos of every style and every color from eight different angles, to help the customer visualize the product better. Zappos.com has also categorized the products that help the customer narrow down their search quickly; for example, if you are looking for women's shoes, you can quickly select the type you want (like casual or dress), and further narrow down your search based on size, width, comfort level, heel height, price, color, manufacturer, accents, pattern and material. This helps the customer sort through thousands of women's shoes to find something they prefer. Also, free overnight shipping ensures that the shoes are delivered to the customer's doorstep very quickly. In Fact, one in every 60 overnight shipments with UPS is from Zappos.com. And if the shoes do not meet the customer's demands, they can be shipped back for free as well. All these factors make it convenient for the customer to shop with Zappos.com (Convenience).

The Quality and Fashion factors of the customer experience are controlled by product suppliers and are not the key focus of Zappos.com, though they make sure they offer attractive and high-quality shoes on their website. They feature an ordinary customer experience on the Quality and Fashion factors. Price is likewise not a factor that the company focuses on, as the customer segment that shops with them is not as price-sensitive; hence, it delivers an ordinary experience on the Price factor.

Overall, Zappos.com delivers a best-in-class customer experience on five factors — Service/Support, Brand, Requirements, Availability and Convenience — that matter the most to its target customer segment.

Up until now, we have seen examples of consumer-focused e-commerce companies entering crowded marketplaces, differentiating themselves from their competitors, and shifting the market away from the incumbents. Just like these successful companies, innovators should analyze the customer experience delivered by the competition and look for ways to differentiate themselves on the factors that matter most to their target customer segment.

Next, let us see how a telecom company in Kenya has disrupted the banking industry by providing mobile banking to the Kenyan people. This is a great case file which shows that by just delivering a good customer experience, a company can enter into an entirely different industry and shift the market in its favor.

Mobile Banking

Kenya had poor banking infrastructure in 2006, with fewer than 600 bank branches and fewer than 800 ATMs[28] in a country with a population of 34 million and many citizens who were unbanked (i.e., did not use any banking system). This was because most of bank branches and ATMs were located in densely populated urban areas, while farmers living in rural areas did not have much access to any bank. If a farmer had to use a bank, he would have to travel long distances to get to a branch or an ATM; this was risky, as the chances of getting robbed on the way back from the bank were high. So they choose not to use the banking system and store their money under a mattress. This led to further problems for the farmer: the risk of theft always worried the farmer, and he could not develop any financial history in order to get loans from the banking system. This meant that he would have to rely on local peasants for loans, and they would charge exorbitant interest rates.

---

[28] Regulations and Supervisions of Bank Channels – Policy Options for Kenya – January 2010 by FSD Kenya

There was another problem facing people living in rural Kenya who had family working far away in urban centers: there was no efficient and inexpensive way for their families to send money to them. The options were to either pay a big fee to send the money using the postal service, or to request someone, usually a friend and often a bus driver, to deliver the money. This method was risky, as the courier might never deliver the money to the intended recipients.

This was a big social issue for Kenya, but not much could be done to fix it due to a poor banking infrastructure. This remained the case until Safaricom, the largest cell phone operator in Kenya, saw that its prepaid users were using airtime minutes to pay for goods and services. Since the prepaid minutes were as good as cash, the users would transfer them from one phone to the other as a form of payment. This motivated Safaricom to start a new mobile banking service called M-Pesa (M stands for mobile and *pesa* means "money" in Swahili.

When M-Pesa was launched in 2007, the initial concept was to develop it as a microfinance network, where users could borrow and repay small loans, but soon Safaricom pivoted to support mobile financial transactions. Anyone with a valid national ID or passport could go to a Safaricom agent and register to use M-Pesa. These are regular retail agents that sell airtime and many other goods to their customers. Registered M-Pesa users could deposit or withdraw money with the agents, who earn commission on such transactions. They could also use the money in their accounts to buy airtime, pay bills, pay other people and send money to family in rural areas.

This mobile payment model completely disrupted the banking industry in Kenya, and made it easier and more secure for Kenyans to deal with money. The irony is that M-Pesa is operated by a company that is not registered as a banking institution, but rather the country's largest mobile service provider.

Safaricom has experienced significant growth with M-Pesa. At the beginning of 2012, there were about 17 million registered M-Pesa users[29], about 40 percent of Kenyan population. By September 2012, M-Pesa had close to 46,000 agents across Kenya, many more than the number of ATMs and bank branches combined. Safaricom revenues from M-Pesa for the first three quarters of 2012 were close to $120 million (10.4 billion Kenyan shillings, or KSh)[30], about 18 percent of Safaricom revenues. In the five years since its inception, M-Pesa has completed KSh 1.5 trillion worth of transactions, and monthly transaction value is around KSh 56 billion. The lowest value of a transaction is KSh 10 and the highest is KSh 70,000[31]. These numbers are staggering for a five-year-old initiative, and this model is being replicated in other countries by mobile operators.

Let us discuss some key factors of customer experience delivered by M-Pesa to understand the reasons behind this astounding growth. Figure 11 shows the customer experience delivered by M-Pesa.

A September 2008 survey, conducted by William Jack of Georgetown University and Tavneet Suri of MIT Sloan, found that M-Pesa has 2.5 times more transactions than regular bank transactions in Kenya — 100,000 transactions for M-Pesa compared to 40,000 bank check transactions. But the financial value of transactions per day was much smaller for M-Pesa — KSh 0.1 billion for M-Pesa compared to KSh 8.5 billion for bank

---

[29] http://en.wikipedia.org/wiki/M-Pesa

[30] Vodafone takes home Sh1bn of M-Pesa Revenue by Mark Okutah; Posted Thursday November 8, 2013; http://www.businessdailyafrica.com/Corporate+News/Vodafone+takes+home+Sh1bn+of+M+Pesa+revenue+/-/539550/1615422/-/2d3k5h/-/index.html

[31] Safaricom 5 year statistics: https://squaddigital.com/beta/safaricom/facebook/saftimelineiframe/pdf/infograph.pdf

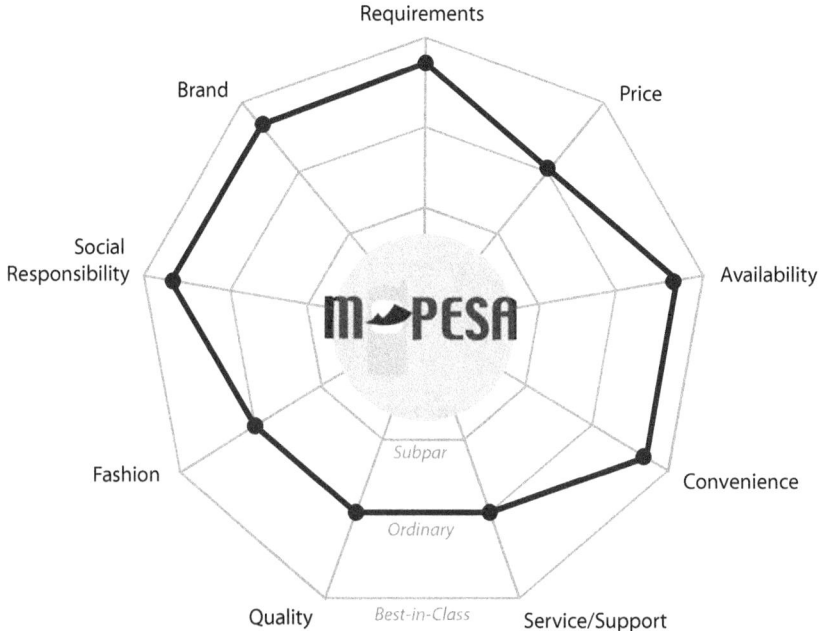

Figure 11: M-Pesa Customer Experience

checks[32]. This shows that M-Pesa users were using its services to transfer small amounts of money from one person to the other, a niche that banking institutions within Kenya did not know existed.

So why was this service used for such small money transfers?

To understand this, let us review the security conditions in Kenya. It is not safe for most people to carry cash with them, as they run a risk of getting robbed. By using M-Pesa, they have access to a method of paying without taking on the risk of carrying cash, so they started using the service to pay for taxi rides, goods and services, and utility bills.

---

[32] Economics of M-Pesa – William Jack, Georgetown University and Tavneet Suri, MIT Sloan; August 2010.

They also started using M-Pesa to send money home to rural areas, because it was fast, reliable and more economical then the postal services or the bus driver that used to deliver the money.

From this, we understand that the prime requirement for Kenyan people, both banked and unbanked, was security and the ability to transfer money over long distances. In fact, 26 percent of the people who took the survey in September 2008 reported that safety was their main motivation for using the service. This requirement was not being fulfilled by the Kenyan banking system, but was done very well by M-Pesa, so it delivered a best-in-class customer experience on the Requirements factor.

Next, consider the customer experience delivered on the Price factor. Safaricom has published fees per transaction, which start at KSh 3 and can go all the way up to KSh 175[33]. Though these are published tariffs, they can change at any point in time — in fact, in 2012, Safaricom reviewed and changed their tariff structure, which meant that users paid higher commissions on amounts over KSh 3,500. There has also been a push from the agents to charge for more transactions. Though the tariffs paid by the user is the lowest for money transfers, the customer experience delivered to the users on the Price factor is ordinary, as the user could get a surprise increase in transaction fees at any point.

There are about 45,000 M-Pesa agents throughout the country, more than the total number of ATMs and bank branches. These agents serve as cash-in/cash-out outlets for M-Pesa users, and are easily accessible in both urban and rural areas. Hence, M-Pesa delivers a best-in-class customer experience on the Availability factor.

---

[33] M-Pesa tariffs:
http://www.safaricom.co.ke/personal/m-pesa/m-pesa-services-tariffs/tariffs

In the September 2008 survey conducted by Jack and Suri, 45 percent of users reported that M-Pesa was very easy to use, as people can transfer money to their family members at anytime they want and the money is credited into their account almost immediately. It has also become much easier for people to pay bills and pay for services, like taxi drivers, barbers, and the like, so M-Pesa delivers a best-in-class customer experience on the Convenience factor.

Safaricom is the largest mobile operator in Kenya and has the Brand value to support such a service, delivering a best-in-class customer experience on the Brand factor.

Let us examine the Social Responsibility factor, and how M-Pesa has an impact on this factor. Poor banking infrastructure made it difficult for people to save money in Kenya; often, the money was stored under a mattress or in some other similar place. After M-Pesa was launched, people started using it for saving money as well. They would deposit money into their account and leave it there, as it was secure and they could access it at any time. Availability of this service has increased the overall savings rate in Kenya. The service has also increased the number of financial transactions between people, making it easier for them to earn and spend money. The African Development Bank (AfDB) claims that M-Pesa has involved more people into the financial sector, and may have contributed to the 19.7 percent inflation rate in the country[34]. This means that M-Pesa has given the power to save and spend money to many Kenyans, positively impacting their quality of life and delivering a best-in-class customer experience on the Social Responsibility factor.

---

[34] M-Pesa linked to rise in Inflation – Money Markets – by George Ngigi - http://www.businessdailyafrica.com/M-Pesa-linked-to-rise-in-inflation/-/539552/1327538 /-/13rogmr/-/index.html

Safaricom realized that many of its customers were using M-Pesa to save money, so in December 2012 they started a new banking product called M-Shwari, which allows them to save and borrow money right from their phone. It even pays interest on the money saved using this service. In its first month of operations, it has collected over KSh 976 million in savings and has granted loans of over KSh 123 million. This is incredible progress, and we can hope that M-Shwari improves Kenyan citizens' access to money.

M-Pesa and M-Shwari are great examples of customer experience-driven innovation, where a telecom provider with no banking background was able to provide banking services to its users and quickly make its mark in the banking industry.

The heavily regulated and frigid banking industry needs such disruptions. Imagine a construction worker in Dubai being able to send money back to family in Indonesia using his cell phone. Imagine a Mexican worker in California paying utility and grocery bills for her family in rural Mexico without leaving her house. Services like these will bring a lot of flexibility, control and efficiency for the users; but unfortunately they cannot be implemented today because of regulations and poor banking infrastructure. One day, though, some innovator could disrupt this market and shift it away from the current incumbents. Until then, users will have to live with the bad customer experience they get from the status quo.

In the next chapter, we will review more successful customer experience-driven innovation examples within the B2B setting.

· **CHAPTER 4** ·

Business-Focused Innovation

Networking Industry Innovation

Consider the story of a client of mine from the networking equipment industry, a company that makes switches and routers used by businesses to provide high speed internet within their office buildings, on campuses and to their customers. We will call it "ChallengerCo" to maintain confidentiality.

At one point, ChallengerCo was trying to win a multi-million-dollar international deal competing against the 800-pound gorilla in the industry, or "market leader". The customer wanted to have a good alternative to the market leader and it invited ChallengerCo in for discussions.

After the first couple of meetings, the customer was pleasantly surprised by ChallengerCo's technology and knew that it would meet their Requirements. They took some references to check on the Quality of ChallengerCo's equipment and found it to be reliable — in fact, they found that the networking equipment from the ChallengerCo had a useful life of 7 to 10 years, far longer than the typical network refresh time of 3 - 5 years, i.e. the time after which they would replace their networking equipment. This opened the doors for ChallengerCo, and the customer added it to their list of approved vendors.

The discussions about this multi-million-dollar deal started to pick up steam as the customer shared the blueprints of their network architecture and their future plans for expansion. During these intense technology and business discussions, ChallengerCo sent in the best of its sales, engineering, corporate development, finance and support staff to meet with the customer. This helped them build deep relationships across the customer's organization and build Brand value for the company. Everyone was very hopeful that this deal would take their game to the next level and give them enough credibility and Brand recognition to compete against the market leader.

Once there was enough trust and sufficient relationships established with the customer, the discussion steered towards Price. ChallengerCo was willing bend over backwards to win this deal, so they put the best of their minds on the task and designed three financing options for the customer.

Option one was a heavily discounted Price for which the customer would have to pay cash to purchase the equipment. Option two was a zero-percent financing option, where ChallengerCo would lend money to finance the deal and provide the equipment at no interest to the customer. Option three was to provide the equipment on a three-year lease with attractive payment and end-of-lease terms. None of these options met the profit thresholds for ChallengerCo, but it was willing to make less money, as it believed that this deal would open doors to future multi-million-dollar international deals which, up to that point, were pretty much reserved for the market leader.

After working with the customer on a few iterations of the three options, a final version was submitted. The customer acknowledged receipt of the final proposal and promised to get back within a week with a decision. Everyone at ChallengerCo waited anxiously for the customer's response; they were very optimistic and had already started planning for a big celebratory dinner. The sales representatives were busy negotiating the big commission checks they would get for closing the deal.

A week went by, with still no response from the customer. ChallengerCo waited patiently for another week but did not hear back, so the sales representatives started probing the customer for the reasons behind the delay, only to find that the market leader was blocking the deal.

Most of the customer's IT staff had been trained in using the market leader's equipment and were not comfortable with the ChallengerCo deal, as they did not want to learn how to use different equipment. They had tipped off the market leader, which was now attempting to prevent the deal from going through.

The market leader had a strong reputation in the industry, and was using this strong Brand value to their advantage. In fact, there was a saying that no one ever got fired for buying the market leader's equipment. It also had a lot of cash it was siphoning out to its finance arm, so it did not have to deal with third-party banks and could provide very attractive financing terms to its customers.

Four weeks after ChallengerCo submitted its proposal, the market leader submitted its own and won the deal. The market leader had an advantageous position across the Brand and Price factors of the customer experience, and it could keep strengthening its position as long as it kept ChallengerCo and other small competitors away from wining these big deals.

This is not the first time this has happened in the industry, or the only industry where the market leader pulls out all the stops to suppress the ChallengerCos. Market leaders typically have considerable resources that can help them win any sizable deal, as loss of market share has a negative impact on their share price and, eventually, on executive payouts.

In the example above, ChallengerCo had just three employees working on financing all of their deals, while the market leader had that many people working on just this one deal. By employing significant resources on major deals, market leaders ensure that they win most sizable and strategic deals, while the smaller deals are left for the minor players in the industry. This was very much ChallengerCo's experience, as they felt restricted to smaller deals.

Frustrated by the defeat, ChallengerCo set out to learn how it could differentiate itself from the market leader and deliver a better customer experience. They were equal on the Requirements and Quality factors of the customer experience, but the market leader could deliver a much better Brand and Price-related customer experience.

Figure 12 highlights the customer experience differences between ChallengerCo and the market leader.

In its quest to deliver a better customer experience, ChallengerCo started exploring every other factor to figure out where it could differentiate against the market leader.

For multi-million-dollar B2B networking equipment deals, Availability is seldom a meaningful customer experience factor, as it takes months to install the equipment and put it into service. This gives enough time for the vendor to manage their operations and deliver the equipment by agreed-upon dates to the customer. There is not much anyone can do to deliver a differentiated customer experience on this factor. ChallengerCo even played with the idea of delivering all the equipment at once while only charging the customer when they started using the equipment. This did not work well for the customer, as they did not have enough storage space to store all

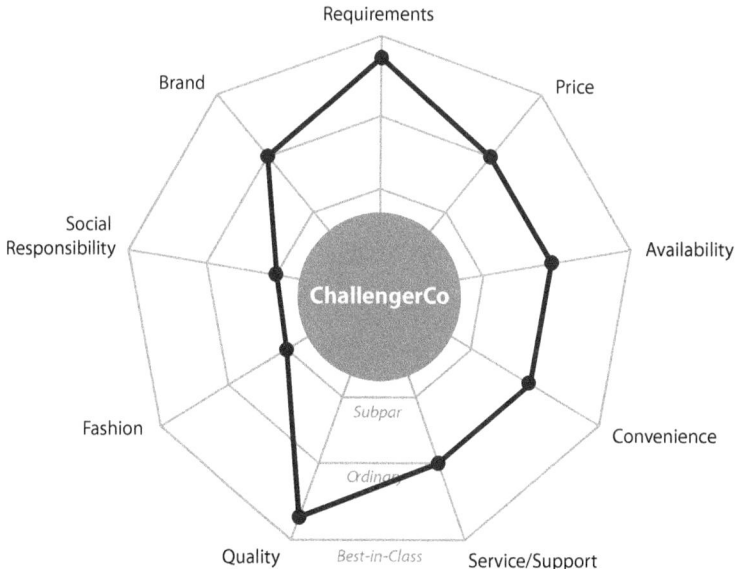

Figure 12: Customer Experience Comparison for Networking Equipment Industry

the equipment, so they wanted the ChallengerCo to deliver the equipment when they were ready to install it and charge them on delivery.

Service/Support is part of the service-level agreement, and the customers pay yearly maintenance fees for this experience. Although ChallengerCo had some Price advantage on its Service/Support fees, the market leader provided a good enough customer experience on this factor. Moreover, customers in the industry do not make a multi-million-dollar equipment purchase decision based on few thousand dollars worth of Service/Support agreement, so there was not much opportunity to differentiate on that factor.

Fashion and Social Responsibility have no impact in the networking equipment industry. As most of the equipment is locked up in the data center or in a closet somewhere. Certain vendors do advertise their equipment to be power-efficient and hence socially responsible, but in the long run, this is more of a cost savings experience for the customer than an environmental sustainability (Social Responsibility) one.

The only factor, then, where ChallengerCo could differentiate itself from the market leader was the Convenience factor. But consider the difficulties involved here: the equipment is often bulky, requires professional installation and is kept in a well air-conditioned facility. So there were not many alternative options in terms of how the equipment could be procured, installed and maintained. Additionally, trained professionals are required to monitor and maintain the equipment, and the majority of these are certified on the market leaders equipment.

Just when the hopes of achieving any kind of differentiation were wearing thin, ChallengerCo came across a new international accounting rule that was being debated by many of the big corporations. Given the global nature of American companies, there was a proposal on the table to move U.S.

accounting rules from the Generally Acceptable Accounting Principles (GAAP) to the International Financial Reporting Standards (IFRS). One particular change in the rule involved lease accounting, where American corporations could no longer expense their leases; they were being forced to capitalize leased equipment and depreciate it over a period of time. There was a considerable amount of unhappiness expressed by many US corporations in regards to this rule change.

It dawned on ChallengerCo that accounting for expensive networking equipment is a pain point for customers, especially when the expense hits the balance sheet. This creates additional work for their accounting teams and increases compliance risk if they do not depreciate the equipment using the right methodology.

Asset tracking is also a big pain point which requires customers to tag all networking equipment, track it on a periodic basis, and report the status of assets on a quarterly basis. The Sarbanes-Oxley Act (SOX) and other accounting regulations mandate that companies track the equipment to make sure that it is in working condition and still owned by the company. In cases where the equipment is lost or is no longer usable, companies need to realize an accounting loss in their financial statements. Failure to follow proper asset tracking procedures could lead to compliance risk for the company, and they could be forced to rework their financial statements. This is a huge operational nightmare for many executives at big corporations.

These pain points were created because of U.S. accounting requirements, and publicly traded companies were facing costs and risks due to these requirements. The adoption of international accounting rules was going to elevate the pain further, as accounting rules were getting even stricter.

The opportunity for ChallengerCo, then, was to make it convenient for their customers by not having to worry about accounting, tracking or reporting the equipment. To solve these pain points, ChallengerCo designed a "Subscription Program" that would allow customers to rent the equipment on a monthly basis, without any contracts or penalties. The customer would pay a monthly fee for using the equipment and return it when they no longer wished to pay the fee.

There were considerable advantages for the customer from this Subscription Program, as the equipment would not be owned or leased by them, and thus would not show up on their balance sheet — freeing them from the obligation to track or report it. Because there are no contracts or early-term cancellation fees, the accounting rules cannot estimate the dollar value of the equipment used by the customer, and the accounting rules cannot force the customer to capitalize the equipment. The customer has to make sure they keep making monthly payments for the time they use the equipment, and return it when they do not need it anymore. This was designed to make it convenient for customers to procure and use the networking equipment, thus delivering a best-in-class experience on the Convenience factor.

This program also had an additional impact on the customer experience, specifically for cash-strapped customers who are unable to buy the equipment or get good loan terms. Since there was no contract or penalties, these customers would bear no financial risk for procuring the equipment. For them, the program provided the best customer experience on the Price factor in the short term.

After designing the Subscription Program, ChallengerCo decided to interview a few different customers to validate its benefits. They assumed that this program was not beneficial to all customer segments, and wanted to confirm their assumption. They were right: some customers were not at all interested in this idea, but others were willing to sign multi-million-dollar deals.

First, they interviewed customers who were cash-rich and had very little debt. They were not especially attracted by this initiative, as they preferred to buy their equipment for cash. They had efficient accounting processes and well-trained staff who could track, report and account their equipment, so the program was not beneficial to them, so they were not the target segment.

Then ChallengerCo talked to customers who were cash-rich, but for whom networking equipment was the greatest part of their business expenditure. These customers had lot of variability in their networking equipment usage; they would spend large amounts of cash buying the equipment to meet their peak demand and it would sit idle for the majority of the year. On top of this, they were finding it difficult to track, report and maintain it throughout the year. Also, they had a desire for the latest technology on their network, which meant that they were in a continuous cycle of buying and recycling equipment. This caused the customers a lot of pain, as they spent significant time and resources on tasks that added little value to their business. They were looking for a program that could provide them with some flexibility and free up their cash reserves and resources.

These customers really liked the program, and struck a deal to pay ChallengerCo only when the equipment was being used. They also had the option to exchange the equipment for newer versions when they were released on the market. ChallengerCo had carefully designed this program so that it could take on all the risk and still meet its profitability targets, so they were ready to meet the needs of this customer segment. Initially, ChallengerCo had forecasted a few hundred-thousand-dollar deals with this customer segment, but the very first was a multi-year, multi-million-dollar deal.

Then there were cash-strapped government agencies that did not have the budgets to buy any more equipment, but had the need to replace their old, outdated technology. They also spent a lot of resources on tagging the equipment and tracking it for reporting government assets. They were also paying huge fees to the market leader for maintaining all the old equipment.

The Subscription Program was well-received by these agencies, as they did not need a purchase budget (for which they need approvals) to get newer equipment, but could pay for the equipment using their approved expense budget. They would also cut down expenses related to tracking this equipment, reporting it on a monthly basis and maintaining the old technology. Given the benefits of this program, government agencies also placed a multi-million-dollar order to upgrade their older networking equipment.

The customer experience delivered by the program is shown in Figure 13.

Given that this program delivered better customer experience by making it convenient for customers to account for and manage their assets, and made the equipment affordable to cash-strapped customers, it was successful on launch. It generated significantly higher sales than initial forecasts, and most deals were multi-million-dollar deals.

This is a great example of how an underdog in the industry was able to punch above its weight by focusing on delivering a better customer experience. The odds were always against the underdog, as the market leader had insurmountable power and Brand value, but the market leader did not deliver a best-in-class customer experience on factors that were important to the customers. By doing so, the underdog was able to win.

In this example, we saw how focusing on the customer experience can

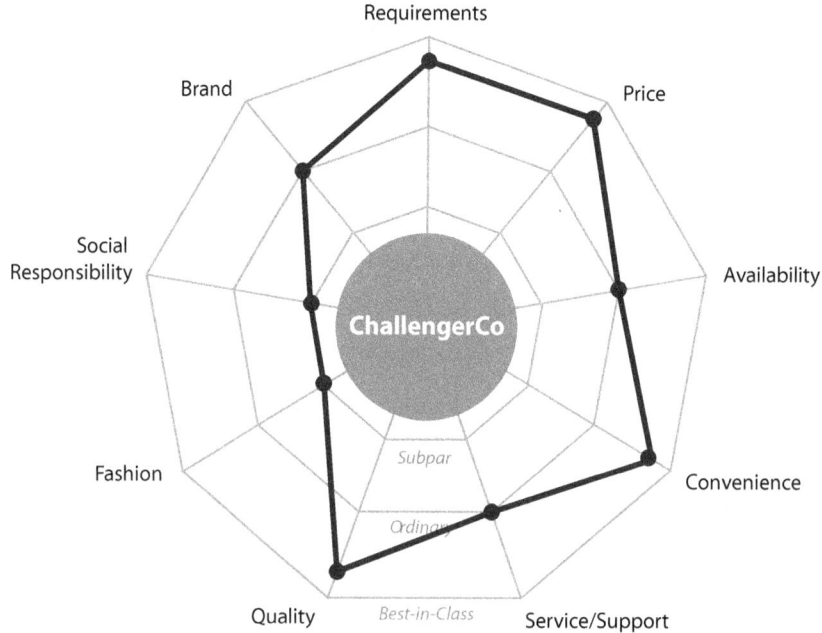

Figure 13: Subscription Services Program Customer Experience

help the underdog shift the market in its favor. But what about cases where the market has not been established, and you are one of the front-runners trying to define it? Delivering good customer experience is even more important in this scenario, as we will see in the next example.

Mobile Marketing Innovation

The Launch of Hipcricket

Back in 2004, broadcasting stations were finding it difficult to justify the return on advertisement dollars spent on radio programming, as there was no way to measure the impact of radio marketing campaigns. In many cases, it was difficult to pinpoint the number of listeners who had actually heard an ad and made a purchasing decision. In the internet age, when immediate interactions with customers are possible and the return on ad dollars is easily calculated, it was becoming difficult for radio stations to compete for top ad dollars, so they needed some way to improve their interaction with listeners and get them engaged in specific marketing campaigns.

Back then, Graham Knowles and Iain Simms found a way to solve this challenge. Their idea was to have radio station anchors ask listeners to send text messages (SMS) to a particular short code — a form of SMS telephone number — and receive coupons and promotional offers in return. This could help marketers measure their campaigns, as they would know the number of listeners who responded with text messages, how many coupons were sent out, and the number of coupons used — and, hence, the additional business generated by the campaign. This could solve the challenge of calculating the return on ad dollars spent on radio programming.

Graham and Iain shared this idea with Ivan Braiker, a broadcasting industry executive, who immediately saw its potential. This was not only powerful for marketers, but also helped radio channels know how many active listeners they had and what their preferences were, such as which marketing campaigns interested them most, what times of the week they tuned in, and what programs they liked.

With this powerful idea as the foundation, Ivan, Graham and Iain launched Hipcricket that same year. From the beginning, Ivan was committed to building a company that would deliver the best possible customer experience. His role as a co-founder involved using his broadcasting industry connections to secure initial meetings with radio station executives, and he got a few that resulted in a few customers willing to try out the technology.

The results of their initial tests were astounding. Radio anchors would ask listeners to text back to win tickets or coupons, and got a decent response; this opened up a new interaction channel between the radio stations and their audience. As word spread, more and more stations expressed an interest in using this method to interact with their customers. Hipcricket had the right technology, tailored to meet the specific interaction needs of broadcasting stations, and it delivered a best-in-class customer experience on the Requirements factor.

The full customer experience model with respect to Hipcricket's service to broadcasting stations across all factors is shown in Figure 14.

Although Hipcricket had the right solution, it hit a wall when it came to discussions about price. At that time, their pricing was based on the number of SMS received, and the broadcasting executives did not know how to estimate a final cost in advance of a campaign being launched. They worried that if they got millions of SMS from their listeners, it would exceed their budgets, so they asked Hipcricket to change their pricing structure.

Being a customer experience-focused company, Hipcricket changed their pricing from price-per-SMS to a price-per-campaign model, which was well received by the broadcasting stations. With this new pricing model, Hipcricket delivered a best-in-class customer experience on the Price factor, as the broadcasting stations were able to anticipate their final bill for the campaign before it was launched.

Hipcricket got the right SMS short code for the broadcasting station, and made sure that it worked with different mobile service providers. They also took care of storing, analyzing and responding to all the SMS and the security of the data collected during the campaign. By providing this level of service, Hipcricket made it convenient for the broadcasting

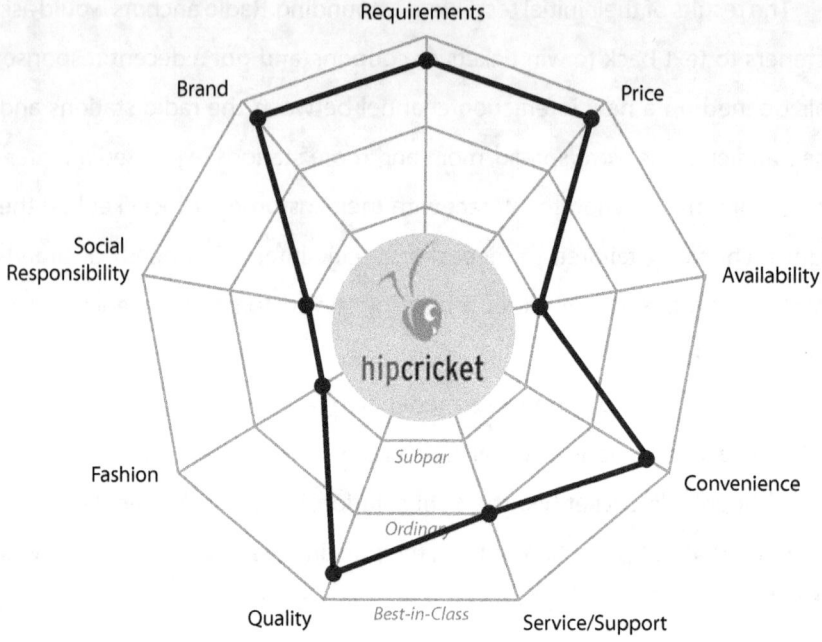

Figure 14: Customer Experience Delivered by Hipcricket to Broadcasters

stations to use them, delivering a best-in-class customer experience on the Convenience factor.

Why did Hipcricket deliver a subpar customer experience on the Availability factor? Between 2004 and 2006, text messaging hadn't yet taken off as a communication channel except with teenagers, and the radio stations had a different demographic. It was only after 2006 that SMS adoption took off across the broader population in the U.S.

Hipcricket always strived to provide good Service/Support and made sure they had account managers and service staff ready to help their customers. This was not a big differentiator for the company, however, as it was offered by other companies doing business with broadcasters. This is why the customer experience delivered by Hipcricket on the Service/Support factor is shown as ordinary.

The marketing campaign data stored by Hipcricket contained confidential information about radio listeners, which was of concern to broadcasters as many of their competitors were on Hipcricket as well. To address these concerns, Hipcricket made sure that account managers and customer services reps were not reused across competing broadcasting stations. They secured their databases to ensure that listener data and information from one radio station was not accidentally leaked to a competing station. This ensured a level of comfort for the broadcasters and delivered a best-in-class customer experience across the Quality factor.

Last but not least, Ivan had good relationships with the CEOs of many broadcasting stations. These relationships helped Hipcricket deliver a best-in-class customer experience across the Brand factor. Without it, the CEOs of radio stations would not have felt comfortable trying some new technology on the air.

The best-in-class customer experience delivered by Hipcricket reaped considerable rewards for the company, as it became the leading mobile marketing service provider for over 100 broadcasters across the country.

Pivot to Mobile Marketing

Though Hipcricket was doing well in the broadcasting industry, its overall growth prospects were limited when compared to its audacious revenue and profit goals, so Ivan and his team started exploring other avenues to grow more aggressively. This is when they stumbled across mobile marketing space. The idea here was to sell their services to major brands across the country and help them connect with customers through mobile marketing.

Smartphones are the fastest growing technology segment, with 48.1 percent of US cell phone subscribers owning a smartphone[35]. Mobile media consumption has been on the rise as well, with 47.6 percent of subscribers using mobile apps and 47.5 percent using mobile browsers. This growth in usage is very exciting to marketers, as it opens another channel they can use to interact with their target audiences. Furthermore, this marketing channel is location-aware, which means that users can be sent a promotional offer or a marketing message when they are close to a particular store. This increases the chances of the customer trying out or purchasing a product or service.

If you are a frequent traveler and have opted in for Blue Moon Beer marketing communication by downloading their app, the next time you land in the Dallas airport you will get a message on your cell phone about the closest restaurant serving Blue Moon beer. You might also get a coupon for appetizers at that restaurant. This increases the chances of your going to that restaurant and ordering Blue Moon beer with your appetizers.

Additionally, mobile marketing can be used by stores to interact with you while you are shopping. Imagine you are at Macy's and are interested in buying some clothes for your spouse. You are right next to the Tommy Hilfiger clothing aisle, but you are not sure about the brand or their style. There is a marketing message in the area with a matrix bar code called Quick Response (QR) code. You scan this code using your cell phone, and immediately, it will download a video about the Tommy Hilfiger clothing line. At the end of the video, you might get a coupon, which could be used to get a discount on Tommy Hilfiger clothing products. You like the product and the discount is pretty hard to turn down, so you pick a pair of jeans and walk out to the

[35]comScore's "2012 Mobile Future in Focus" report summary by MarketingProfs
http://www.marketingprofs.com/charts/2012/7236/key-mobile-marketing-stats-and-trends-for-2012

counter. As soon as you complete your purchase, you get another coupon from Macy's for purchasing a polo shirt that goes along well with the Tommy Hilfiger jeans. So instead of getting out of the store you continue shopping, and purchase more items. This is location-aware marketing, where a company interacts with you to deliver information and promotional offers to influence your purchasing decision right in the store.

Mobile marketing and advertising is still a nascent industry, but it is growing fast as more and more brands realize that it is an effective marketing channel. Unfortunately, many brands do not know how to use this new channel, so they look for outside help in designing, launching and measuring their mobile campaigns. This provided the next big opportunity for Hipcricket.

Hipcricket wanted to be the company that enables brands to provide this type of location-aware interactive marketing to mobile users, but their SMS-based technology was not sufficient to fulfill that vision. They needed to expand their technology to offer all types of mobile media, including mobile ads, SMS, QR codes, mobile sites and other applications. This would enable them to move beyond broadcasting stations and start working with bigger brands on their mobile marketing campaigns. They invested in building the remaining pieces of the technology, started supporting all types of mobile platforms and mobile carrier networks, and rebranded themselves as a mobile marketing and advertising company, and started targeting big brands.

But the expectations of this customer segment were much different than those of the broadcast stations. This segment was much more data and technology-savvy, so they demanded real-time access to campaign data. They also wanted the ability to make real-time changes to the campaign based on the data they were gathering. For example, a 50 percent discount coupon on apparel could be dialed down to a lesser discount if there was a tremendous response to the campaign. Likewise, a campaign that was not doing well could be ramped up with different offers. Hipcricket, at that time, did not have the capability to offer such real-time access and modifications, but they learned about their customer requirements and built the technology to provide such access.

Brands were accustomed to using different marketing channels in the past, including radio, TV and internet, so they understood the regulations with these marketing channels. Mobile marketing, on the other hand, was a new channel for them, and they did not understand the regulatory risks involved. These risks are significant, as anti-spam laws are very stringent and brands have paid substantial fines for spamming mobile users. In 2008, Timberland shoes set aside $7 million to pay $150 to each customer who received an unauthorized text message from the company[36]. Similarly, Twentieth Century Fox and FoxStore.com were sued for sending unauthorized text messages announcing the release of the movie *Robots* on DVD. They set aside $16 million to settle the lawsuit, which amounted to $200 per text message.

Even though mobile is a lucrative marketing channel, it can become a very expensive one if you don't know how to make the best use of it. So these brands were looking for partners they could trust to guide them through the regulatory landscape. Hipcricket saw this as an opportunity, spent time and effort to understand all the details of the regulatory environment, and built a product that actively manages the risks involved in mobile marketing.

Hipcricket knew that the brands needed someone who could be their one-stop end-to-end mobile marketing and advertising partner. So they gained all the capabilities required to be that partner, and started providing a variety of services and solutions to customers. To start with, they provide

---

[36] SMS Spam Lawsuite By Derek Johnson - http://www.tatango.com/blog/sms-spam-lawsuits/

strategic services that help customers understand the mobile marketing land-scape. It works with the customers, lists out their mobile marketing goals, and recommends a solution to meet those goals. It also trains customers on the different aspects of mobile marketing, including rules that can keep the cus-tomers out of trouble — for example, the opt-in authorization, where the mobile users agree to receive mobile messages. Once the mobile user opts in, the companies have to make them aware of any costs involved in receiving the messages. The user also has to acknowledge that she has signed up to receive marketing messages. At the completion of this process, the brands are allowed to send out marketing messages to the customers. The marketer also needs to provide an easy way for the mobile user to opt *out*, and to make sure that the mobile user is removed from their database within ten days of doing so.

These are strict rules that the marketers need to follow; otherwise they can end up with big fines or lawsuits. Hipcricket ensures that its customers are aware of and are trained in all these mobile marketing rules. They might be easy to follow when you have only a few mobile users, but it is an intimidating task to manage national campaigns targeting thousands of users.

Hipcricket's self-service AD LIFE® platform helps customers manage the complex challenges of a marketing campaign. This technology platform pro-vides a suite of tools to reach all types of mobile devices, and to manage the interaction points with mobile users. Using it, customers are able to set up a mobile website that provides product information, send coupons to mobile users, invite them to enter contests, and to opt in for future messaging. The platform also manages the opt-out process for mobile users by completely deleting their information from the database. AD LIFE® also includes real-time analytical tools that help customers measure their campaign results and make changes on the fly to improve the campaign performance.

Let us analyze the customer experience delivered by Hipcricket as shown in Figure 15. First, Hipcricket is an expert in the mobile marketing space and knows the right process to market and advertise to mobile users. This expertise, coupled with their strategic services and training programs, satisfies the knowledge Requirements of the customers. Its AD LIFE® platform provides customers with all the technology options they need to run a successful campaign. Hipcricket's end-to-end solution is one of the best available in the industry today for mobile marketing, reflected in the fact that it has executed more than 200,000 campaigns for more than 600 brands. It also has an over 95 percent renewal rate, which indicates that many of its customers are satisfied with its services. It has received many mobile marketing awards, including the prestigious *Mobile Marketer* Mobile Service Provider of the Year in 2011. This success can be attributed to the best-in-class customer experience provided by Hipcricket on the Requirements factor.

Using Hipcricket's solution, customers can interact with mobile users on any mobile platform, with any mobile service provider. They can use SMS technology, QR codes, mobile websites, games and other ways to interact with customers. The ability to reach all types of mobile users using many different technologies delivers a best-in-class customer experience on the Availability factor. This was the reason behind Hipcricket's winning the Mobile Marketer award in 2011.

Hipcricket's overall solution, including strategic services, training and the technology platform, provides customers with knowledge and technology to be successful with their mobile marketing campaign. This one-stop solution makes it Convenient for the companies to use Hipcricket, delivering a best-in-class customer experience on that factor.

They offer the same level of Service/Support that any B2B company

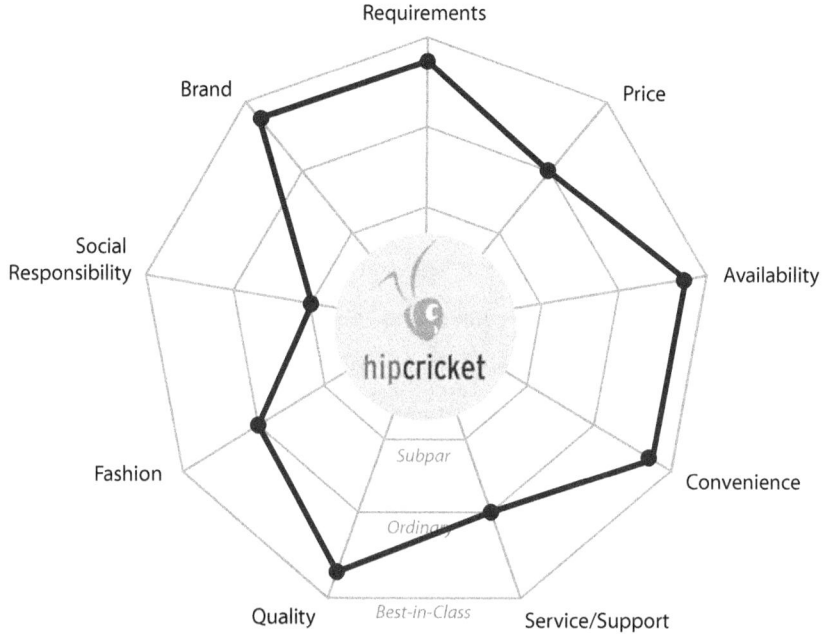

Figure 15: Customer Experience Delivered by Hipcricket to Mobile Marketers

would provide to customers, so their customer experience is ordinary on this factor. But when it comes to the Quality-related customer experience, they are the best-in-class provider, because they have processes to ensure that their customers do not accidentally spam mobile users. They have a strict policy to quickly remove mobile users who have opted out of the marketing campaign, and a process to ensure that all checks have been made before messaging a mobile user who has opted in. Given that they work with so many brands and broadcasting stations, they have built internal processes and organizational structures to ensure that data from one customer does not leak to its competitors. This is essential, as any leak of data could be a strategic blow to its customers.

Now, why does Hipcricket get any rating on the Fashion factor, as they are simply a B2B company that provides customers with a technology platform? This is because their customers consider the ability to manage campaigns on the fly using real-time data to be "cool". Usually marketers design a campaign, test it well, and then launch it to the market. Once it is launched, it is very expensive to change mid-way. But with mobile marketing, they are able change it as often as they like, and this ability is provided by the AD LIFE® platform. However, other providers offer a similar platform, and it is generally expected from any mobile marketing platform; hence, it gets an ordinary rating on this factor.

Hipcricket has managed to build a strong brand in the mobile marketing space. It was one of the finalists in the Mobile Marketing & Advertising Agency of the Year awards, and it won the Most Effective Mobile Campaign award in 2012[37]. It also organizes an annual conference where marketing leaders from all its clients meet and discuss their marketing challenges and solutions. This helps them build a community around their offerings and develops their Brand further. All these efforts ensure that Hipcricket delivers a best-in-class customer experience on the Brand factor.

Hipcricket's focus on delivering a good customer experience saw it grow quickly in a nascent industry. It recently completed 200,000 mobile campaigns, and is experiencing a 52 percent quarter-over-quarter growth. More than 350 customers and 600 brands use Hipcricket for managing their campaigns, including well-known brands like Macy's, MillerCoors, Nestlé and Clear Channel. Hipcricket has emerged as the leader in U.S. mobile marketing and advertising space in only eight years. Due to its success, it was acquired by Augme Technologies for $44.5 million in 2011.

---

[37] Hipcricket awards - http://www.hipcricket.com/awards

Supply Chain Innovation

A lot goes into manufacturing a laptop, from component sourcing and production scheduling to testing and delivery. A production manager at a computer manufacturer needs to manage many moving parts before completing a laptop order. To successfully manufacture a laptop and deliver it on time, the production manager must ensure that all the required components —memory, motherboard, hard drive, laptop case, keyboard, LCD screen, and so on — are available just-in-time during the manufacturing process. Just-in-time (JIT) availability is critical here, because computer manufacturers do not want to stock the components on their factory floor, since any component inventory they carry adds to their cost of operations and reduces profits.

Though JIT reduces inventory costs, it adds risk to the overall schedule, as late or faulty components mean that the production has to stop. To minimize this risk, the production manager needs to have enough substitute components available on hand, in case the preferred supplier is unable to deliver the required quantities on time. Another, less expensive, way to minimize the risk is to have access to information on the supply lines, like where exactly the motherboard orders are, when they will be on the production floor, and how much testing the supplier has done. By having access to this information, the production manager can quickly make decisions that will ensure that the schedule is not interrupted. This is very important, as it helps the production manager minimize costs while ensuring that they meet customer commitments.

One company that makes the makes the lives of production managers easy by providing this information is Taiwan-based contract manufacturer Foxconn.

A few years ago Foxconn invested heavily in IT systems that helped it manage information across its manufacturing and shipping processes. Using these systems, Foxconn tracked the status of orders through every stage of the manufacturing process. Additionally, it could track the status of shipments in detail, such as the shipping date, carrier, which container the product was in, arrival time, who was supposed to clear it from the dock, and the time it would reach the factory floor.

Not only did Foxconn track this information, they shared it with the customer, so the production manager at a computer manufacturer could log in to the Foxconn portal and find all the details about their order. Based on the history of delivery from Foxconn, the manager could then estimate with a high level of confidence when the next order would reach them. This helped the manufacturer to plan the next production run that included the components from Foxconn. By providing all this information, Foxconn delivered a best-in-class customer experience on the Convenience factor to computer manufacturers, as it made it easy for them to plan their production runs when Foxconn was a supplier.

This is a reason why many production managers from computer manufacturers choose Foxconn as their preferred supplier, during a series of interviews conducted by me for one of my clients.

Please read the sidebar to see how customer experience applies to supply chain innovation, and how companies that have managed this well have become the preferred vendors for their customers.

In the next chapter we will discuss how healthcare-focused companies that innovate to deliver a better customer experience, manage to thrive in the industry against all odds. In particular we will learn:

- How one company managed to break into the closed healthcare ecosystem and create a new product category.
- How one organization is using innovative ways to fight bone marrow cancer.
- What the key differences are between the Convenience and Availability factors of customer experience.

· CHAPTER 5 ·

HealthCare Innovation

Portable Ultrasound Innovation

L et us see how an innovative medical devices company shifted the market from traditional ultrasound manufacturers by creating an entirely new product category that delivered a much better customer experience.

Back in April 1998, Kevin Goodwin, CEO and president of Sonosite Inc., was brainstorming with his executives on ways to make a big impact in the market and create a new product category. Their prime focus was to deliver the best customer experience so as to disrupt the industry with this new product and prove all naysayers wrong.

Not too long before, Sonosite Inc. was the Handheld Systems Business Group within American Technology Laboratories (ATL), a market leader in the traditional ultrasound market. It invented a Hand-Carried Ultrasound (HCU) system, which resulted in ATL spinning off the division as a separate company. Being a successful division within ATL was a different game, unlike being a public company with little revenue and little cash. Though this was a time when many internet businesses were going public with high valuation and the market was supportive of new businesses, it still put much pressure on Sonosite team to deliver or be a public failure. Sonosite had a good product at hand in the HCU system, but there was no place for this product in the current market. Radiologists, the primary customers for ultrasound machines, feared that this portable device would disrupt their business, and did not want it to succeed in the market.

There were no other known uses for this portable HCU system. Hospitals and doctor's offices could potentially be a target market segment, but hospitals did not feel the need to use a portable ultrasound device; all of their ultrasound needs were met by their radiologists and ultrasound laboratories. Doctor's offices, meanwhile, were nimble in their operations and did not want the overhead related to buying and maintaining the ultrasound equipment. Sonosite had two options at this point: break into the locked ecosystem owned by the radiologists or create a new product category that would be useful to hospitals and doctor's offices.

Before we dive deeper into Sonosite's challenges with the HCU system any further, let us see how it got here. In 1996, the U.S. government's Defense Advanced Research Projects Agency (DARPA) provided a grant to several companies to develop a portable ultrasound device for use in battlefield conditions. Soldiers are injured in remote locations, and the nearest well-equipped hospital is often hundreds of miles away. At these locations, all injuries, including sprains, muscle tears, fractures and contusions, are treated as emergencies, and the soldier is flown to the nearest hospital; it would be very helpful if there were a way for doctors on the scene to assess the severity of the injury before making a decision. To this end, DARPA provided a grant to develop a portable ultrasound device that was lightweight, easy to use, highly reliable and rugged enough to survive battlefield conditions.

Bothell, Washington-based ATL, which manufactured traditional ultrasound machines, got a $12.6 million matching grant[38], as they had been working on a similar project for about two years. Aided by this grant, ATL increased their research efforts and formed a separate business unit called the Handheld Systems Business Group in 1997. ATL choose Kevin Goodwin to lead this new unit and develop the HCU system, which they delivered within two years.

Success with this project opened up more opportunities for the Handheld Systems Business Group, and Kevin Goodwin wanted to market this device to hospitals and doctors' offices. ATL evaluated the potential opportunities and concluded that it presented far greater risks to the current business. First, the current target customers for ATL were the radiologists, who paid big dollars to buy traditional ultrasound machines for their labs. With the current model, doctors referred their patients to these radiologists, who performed the ultrasound and sent the diagnosis back to the referring doctor. If doctors had access to the HCU Systems and were able to perform ultrasound on their own, it could hurt the business radiologists got from these doctors; gynecologists and cardiologists were already ordering their own ultrasounds and were not referring their patients to radiologists. So these HCU systems threatened the primary target market for ATL — radiologists — and it did not want its brand to be associated with development and marketing of this product.

Second, ATL knew that it would take significant investment to develop this product further for commercial use and to market it to the right audiences. It did not have the required capital to make such an investment. Lastly, Philips was in active discussions to acquire ATL, and it was not interested in

---

[38] Invention to Startup: Sources of Funding. Presentation by Trevor Moody – Frazier Healthcare Ventures and Jens U. Quistgaard – Liposonix Inc.

the Handheld Systems Business Group, as it did not believe the HCU systems had any market potential.

So in April 1998, ATL spun off the Handheld Systems Business Group as Sonosite, with Kevin Goodwin as its President and CEO. They gave Sonosite $17 million in cash, followed by another $13 million at a later stage, and listed it on NASDAQ. ATL was subsequently acquired by Philips for $800 million in September 1998.

Now that Sonosite was in this challenging situation with a newly formed public company and a successful product, it needed to find the market to disrupt. Kevin Goodwin was impressed by Clay Christensen's disruption theory, and called him to help in disrupting the ultrasound market for hospitals. Clay found this to be a sufficiently challenging problem and a great opportunity to prove his theory. Together, they started by focusing on the job that the doctors were trying to do, and how the HCU systems could help them do it better. They conducted primary market research by observing doctors in hospitals, understanding the job they were trying to do, and articulating the desired outcomes and the associated risks. This gave them a clear picture of the job and its related pain points.

While conducting the market research, they found a pain point experienced by doctors: *central line placement*. In this procedure, doctors place a catheter into a large vein found in the neck, chest or groin in order to deliver multiple medications or fluids, or to obtain blood samples; once placed, it could be used to deliver the required medication for weeks. To place this catheter, doctors relied on anatomical landmarks to determine the location of the vein. But every patient is different, and there are anatomical differences in the location of this vein as well; because of these differences, there were unintended accidents with the placement of the central line, like puncturing of the artery that is close to the vein, or puncturing the lung, leading to pneumothorax. Depending on the magnitude of these accidents, it could lead to a severe medical condition for the patient. Doctors were not happy with the blind process of placing a central line and needed visual clues to help them during this procedure. They do this procedure by the patient's bedside, and find it inconvenient to take the patient to a radiology lab or to bring the bulky two hundred-pound ultrasound equipment to the patient's room. So they needed a solution that could be easily transported to the patient's bedside and provide them with visual navigation for placing the central lines.

This was a great use for the lightweight six-pound HCU system, as it could be carried to the patient's bedside and would provide visual clues to the doctors to make sure that the catheter was placed into the right vein. It was like having a guided navigation to the location of the vein, which minimized the probability of the needle puncturing unintended organs. At that time, there were no such solutions available to the doctors, and Sonosite established the initial Requirements for bedside ultrasound. By solving this major pain point for doctors using the HCU systems that could deliver good imaging as well as navigation, Sonosite delivered a best-in-class customer experience on Requirements. This also ensured that they were not competing against the traditional ultrasound manufacturers and were not disrupting the radiologists' business. It was an entirely new product category, serving a market where traditional ultrasound technology could not be used.

Similar use cases, where the doctor had to stick a needle into the patient's body and run the risk of damaging other organs, became a potential market for HCU systems. Anesthesiologists, emergency medicine doctors, and critical care physicians became the golden triangle for Sonosite, as they all could use guided navigation when inserting a needle into a patient's body.

Having established a use for the HCU system (Requirements) for hospitals, Sonosite focused on the other factors of customer experience they would like to deliver. They knew that many doctors and healthcare staff did not know how to use an ultrasound, and this was a barrier to large-scale adoption of their devices. To solve this challenge, they decided to focus on the design of the device to make it "doctor-proof" — technical jargon for making it so easy to use (Convenience) that even a doctor could do so with minimal training. To achieve this goal, they took a less-is-more approach and simplified the features of the portable device. For example, a traditional ultrasound machine has many controls to make numerous measurements, and they also have the ability to run multiple applications simultaneously. None of these complex features were required for the HCU systems, as they would not be used in the target-use cases. So these features were eliminated, which allowed Sonosite to minimize the number of buttons on the machine to a critical few. The thinking was to build a good digital camera with fewer buttons, not a complicated SLR camera. This approach made the HCU systems easy to use and delivered a best-in-class customer experience on Convenience.

Sonosite knew that there were already enough variables that could stress the doctors during the central line placement procedure, and they did not want their equipment to be one of them, so they built a highly reliable device that does not fail in middle of the procedure. These devices get a lot thrown at them, like fluids, blood and alcohol wipes; in addition to being moved around and sometimes dropped, so they need to be rugged and not break easily. The company's experience in building such reliable and rugged devices for naval research helped them in building such a device for hospitals as well; this helped them deliver a best-in-class customer experience on Quality.

Given the portable size of the device, doctors could easily take it into the patient's room and use it while performing the central line procedure by the bedside. Not many devices are as easily accessible; hence, Sonosite managed to deliver a best-in-class customer experience on Availability.

The customer experience delivered by Sonosite during its early years is shown in Figure 16. Although it had a product that could deliver a best-in-class experience across the top four customer experience factors — Requirements, Convenience, Availability and Quality — it still lacked some important factors that are required to sell successfully to hospitals. One such factor was Brand recognition. Hospitals are very risk-averse and tend not to bet their operations on unknown brands. Since Sonosite was a new company, it initially struggled to sell to the hospitals. It built a direct sales team focused on building relationships with the hospitals and delivering the best possible customer experience, but during these early days, their Brand delivered a subpar customer experience, and their Service/Support customer experience was ordinary, even though it promised an excellent level of Service/Support to comfort customers and persuade them to buy the equipment.

There was another problem that faced Sonosite during the early days: convincing the hospitals to spend $15,000 to $50,000 for the HCU system. Only hospitals that had enough cases of unintended accidents that resulted in lawsuits knew the real value of the system, and were thus willing to spend the money to make that purchase. Hospitals with experienced doctors who had used anatomical landmarks for years without accidents did not feel the need to buy the HCU systems. This made non-consumption the biggest competition, as not all doctors felt the need to use this system. Sonosite faced an uphill task of convincing the hospitals about their return on investment, and this led to an ordinary Price-related customer experience.

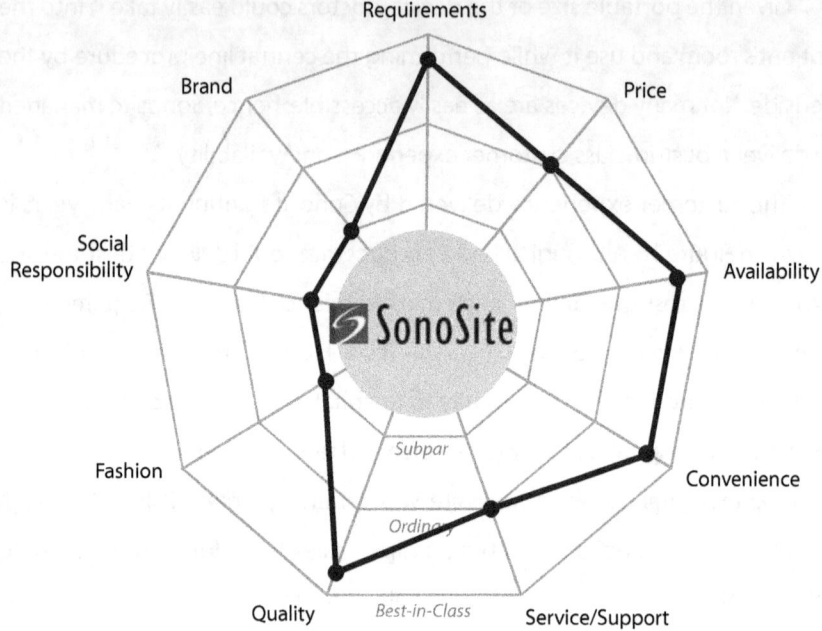

Figure 16: Customer Experience Delivered by Sonosite to Hospitals During Its Early Years

Sonosite delivered a best-in-class customer experience across four factors (Requirements, Availability, Convenience and Quality), an ordinary customer experience on Price, and a subpar customer experience on Brand. Given that it was delivering a good customer experience across four factors that were important to hospitals, it was able to sell its product and slowly build the Brand required to create the new product category.

In 1999, Sonosite started with $10 million in revenues, but by 2002 it had grown to $73 million, close to 100 percent compound annual growth rate (CAGR). By this point, it had attracted the attention of the industry Goliath, GE Healthcare, which saw the potential of the HCU systems product category and launched their own product in 2002. This gave the required legitimacy to this new product category. Over the next few years, GE Healthcare and Sonosite competed aggressively in the global HCU systems marketplace, and given its focus on delivering a best-in-class customer experience, Sonosite retained the market leadership position and developed its Brand.

But Sonosite was not done yet. It stumbled upon an interesting adjacent market, where portable ultrasound could be used to diagnose and treat patients faster. At a leading university, one of the star football players injured his thigh while practicing. The sports medicine doctor for the team recommended rest to recover from the injury, but one week before the big game, the player was still injured with no signs of recovery. This created a lot of anxiety for the team and the coach, as without their star player, their chances of winning were marginal. The sports medicine director of the university was under a lot of pressure to figure out what was wrong with the player as well, and how soon the injury could heal. They could have gotten an MRI or X-ray done, but they did not have the patience to wait two or three days for the results.

This is when the sports medicine doctor got the Sonosite equipment and used it to further diagnose the issue. She was able to see under the player's skin, and found that there was a blood clot in the thigh muscle that was causing the pain. So they took a needle and drained 80 cc blood from the thigh, and this relieved the pain; within a day the player was fit enough to practice. This became a great case study to target sports medicine doctors with Sonosite's musculoskeletal line of product, which is the HCU system used to view the patient's muscular and skeletal system. Using the HCU system, sports medicine doctors could visually observe the extent of a player's injury and recommended the right treatment. In early 2008, Sonosite launched the first of its family of musculoskeletal products, the S-MSK HCU system.

Sports medicine doctors, as a target segment, had a clear pain point in terms of having access to technologies that could be used to diagnose players better and faster. Such diagnoses would help them make quick decisions and come up with alternative treatment if needed. In cases where there was no major injury, it would provide peace of mind to the player and help them stay focused on the sport. It was a great win for both sports medicine doctors and players.

The HCU system provides a best-in-class customer experience on the Availability factor, as the sports medicine doctors could easily carry the unit and have it readily available on the road, during practice sessions, and during the game. They also deliver a best-in-class Convenience-related customer experience, as they are very easy to use. There are educational materials on the best ways to use the system available online[39], which help the customer learn about the product at their own convenience. This made it easier for sports medicine doctors to learn more about the HCU systems and use them in best possible ways to diagnose players.

The flat-rate, one-time Price, with five years of warranty at no additional cost or maintenance contracts, also provides a best-in-class customer experience. This is a departure from the warranty and maintenance terms used by equipment manufacturers within and outside of the healthcare industry. For example, GE Healthcare offers a one-year warranty on hardware and 90 days' warranty on software, which is also the case with most other companies that sell expensive equipment. Usually, such companies also charge 10 percent of the equipment's list price as maintenance fees per year; so on a $40,000 HCU system, GE Healthcare would charge $4,000 per year for warranty and

---

[39] Education material on using the HCU systems is available at:
http://www.sonositeeducation.com

maintenance services after the initial period. Sonosite, on the other hand, provides this service at no additional cost for five years.

Doctors buying Sonosite HCU systems had been worried about theft of the systems due to their small size and light weight. To minimize the anxiety related to theft, Sonosite started offering an upgrade to their warranty program where they would replace a stolen unit. One such incident happened when a doctor reported the unit stolen from the trunk of his car. Sonosite verified the incident and immediately shipped another unit to the doctor. Unfortunately, Sonosite did not have his current address and shipped the unit to a prior address; the doctor did not receive the replacement unit on time and lost business during the time he was waiting for it to arrive. Sonosite took responsibility for shipment errors, and wrote a check to compensate for the lost business. By being so responsive to customer needs, Sonosite delivers a best-in-class customer experience across the Service/Support customer experience as well.

Over the years, Sonosite has also managed to develop the Brand required to make doctors comfortable with the product, and have achieved a position where doctors use "Sonosite" as a verb. But they are still not well-known to the executives of some hospitals, and consolidation of hospitals into large healthcare enterprises continues to threaten the long-term viability of Sonosite. To maintain this strong Brand positioning, Sonosite continues to invest in innovative TV commercials targeting both sports medicine doctors and healthcare enterprises.

The customer experience delivered by Sonosite to all its target customer segments in 2012 is shown in Figure 17.

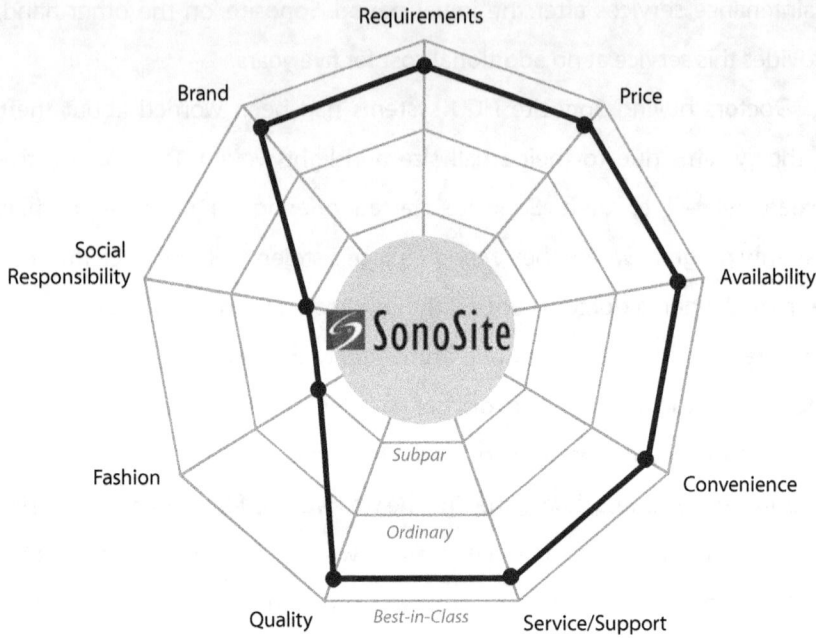

Figure 17: Sonosite Customer Experience in 2012

Sonosite continues to maintain its market leadership position and deliver best-in-class customer experiences on seven of the nine factors — Requirements, Price, Availability, Convenience, Service/Support, Quality and Brand. How does it manage to do this?

To understand this, we should dive into Sonosite's financial performance. In 2011, Sonosite made close to $306 million in revenue with about 70 percent gross margins, which are very healthy for any company. But the cash from operations was close to $2 million, which is only about 0.68 percent. So for all their efforts in 2011, they hardly made any money for their shareholders. If we look further into 2010 and 2009, the issue seems to be the same — close to 70 percent gross margins, but 8 to 9 percent cash from operations. Compare this to their closest competitor, GE Healthcare, whose segment profit from the healthcare industry in 2011 was over 15 percent, with cash from operations for the entire company greater than 22 percent. There are many factors that impact the profitability of a company in a particular year, and it would not be right to conclude that a best-in-class customer experience drives low profitability. Delivering a best-in-class customer experience across any factor is expensive, as it requires both capital and resource commitments, and since Sonosite delivers a best-in-class customer experience across seven factors, it should be that much more expensive, impacting its overall profitability.

How can we be sure that this is indeed the case? To find an answer to this question, we can dig deeper into Sonosite's financial statements. Sonosite reserves close to four percent of its revenues to cover its future warranty liabilities, the money that it intends to use to cover any warranty costs in the future. Its warranty-related costs in 2011 are close to two percent of its revenue, and they fluctuate heavily from year to year, which is the reason for setting aside a warranty liability reserve. Looking into GE's financial statements, its warranty liabilities are closer to one percent of revenues, and 2011 warranty related costs are closer to half a percent of revenues. Sonosite spends four times as much as GE, as a percentage of revenue, for covering the additional four years of warranty that it provides to its customers. This enables it to deliver a best-in-class customer experience on the Price and Service/Support factors of customer experience, but also significantly impacts profit margins. There are many other capital and resource commitments that are required to deliver good customer experience, and they come at a cost to Sonosite. This analysis illustrates that the best-in-class customer experience delivered by Sonosite across seven factors is potentially affecting its bottom line, as it is expensive to deliver such a customer experience.

It would be interesting to see how long Sonosite will be able to maintain this leadership position at such low profit margins. At some point, the desire to make more profits will drive it to reinvent the customer experience it delivers to its customers. Any drastic change that favors profits by reducing levels of customer experience will have a negative impact on its revenues and Brand.

Nonetheless, Sonosite has been successful in creating a new product category, the Hand Carried Ultrasound system, which comprises about 20 percent of the global ultrasound marketplace and is estimated to be at least a $1 billion industry. At the end of 2011, Sonosite was acquired by Fuji Film for $995 million as a strategic investment in this industry. Philips was the other bidder trying to acquire Sonosite, about 13 years after passing up the opportunity to keep the Handheld Systems Business Group within ATL.

Be the Match® Program

In July 2008, a close friend of mine was diagnosed with Acute Myeloid Leukemia (AML), a rare form of life threating blood cancer. His chances of survival depended on finding a bone marrow donor whose genetic makeup matched his. Unfortunately, this process is not that easy, especially if the genetic match is not found within the family. About 70 percent of patients in need of a bone marrow transplant do not find a matching donor within their own family[40]; in fact, some 10,000 patients in the U.S. every year must hope that the healthcare system can find them an outside bone marrow donor. My friend was one of them.

---

[40] National Marrow Donor Program (NMDP) facts and Figures
http://marrow.org/News/Media/Facts_and_Figures_(PDF).aspx

For these patients, life becomes a game of probability where the odds are not in their favor. There are millions of donors registered with the National Marrow Donor Program (NMDP), but finding one whose genetic makeup would match that of my friend was extremely challenging. Like any game of probability, the higher the numbers, the better the chances of finding a match, which is why increasing the number of donors in the database has been one of the primary goals of the NMDP.

In my friend's case, no match was found within the NMDP's database, so his family and close friends started a nationwide donor registration drive in the hope of finding that one donor who would be a good genetic match. The NMDP provided us with the guidance, training and materials required for enrolling new donors into the program. It gave us forms, cheek swabs for collecting donors' genetic information, and marketing materials for promoting the program. We set up booths at local events and talked to hundreds of participants, convincing them to join the donor list.

As these efforts were going on, my friend's condition was getting worse, and we all were concerned that we might lose him. Eventually a donor with a perfect match was found, but it was already too late — he died in November 2008, leaving behind a wife, a five-year-old daughter, and a one-year-old son. We had only a hundred days from the time he was diagnosed with the disease to his passing away; sadly, it wasn't long enough to secure a bone marrow transplant.

Approximately 10,000 patients require a bone marrow transplant each year within the United States alone, but the NMDP is able to provide the perfect match for only 5,500 cases worldwide[41]. Finding matches for all those

---

[41] National Marrow Donor Program (NMDP) facts and Figures
http://marrow.org/News/Media/Facts_and_Figures_(PDF).aspx

who need the right donor in time for a transplant is the challenge that drives NMDP to look for new ways to solve this problem.

The NMDP and its Be The Match Registry® provide the service of matching bone marrow transplant recipients with the right donors. The NDMP is a non-profit organization that was started in 1987 by the federal government, with the social responsibility to maintain the database of donors and find a match for patients in need. It caters to two different types of customers: the donors who trust the NMDP with their contact and genetic information, and its partner networks, which include entities like transplant centers, hospitals, and medical centers. These network partners rely on the NMDP to find the right match for their patients in a timely manner.

Let us first analyze the customer experience delivered by the NMDP to the donors, and why they trust it with their information.

Customer Experience for Donors

At the end of 2011, the NMDP had about 9.5 million donors in its database, which is growing by over 50,000 every month. In 2011 some 650,000 new donors were added. The database also has about 165,000 available cord blood units, which is the blood taken from the umbilical cords of newborn babies and is a rich source of the stem cells required in bone marrow transplants. How does the NMDP manage to find and keep such a large database of donors for such a long period of time? To understand this, let us evaluate the customer experience it delivers to the donors, as shown in Figure 18.

The focus for the NMDP is getting more donors registered, as the probability of finding the perfect match gets better with increasing numbers, so it works diligently on reaching out to people, educating them and convincing them to join the Registry. It conducts marrow drives at local

Figure 18: Customer Experience Delivered by the NMDP to Donors

events and religious institutions, with a focus on educating and registering donors. It also uses social media, including Twitter, Facebook and its own community page, to attract potential donors.

Once it has attracted the attention of a potential donor, the NMDP uses real-life case studies to appeal to the "Good Samaritan" within each of us. For example, in my friend's case, we used pictures of his young family to appeal to potential donors to register. We also had a YouTube video where my friend described his situation and requested people to register with the NMDP. This works well, as it effectively uses a single case to emotionally move the donor to take action, instead of trying to show them statistics on cases where a match is not found. It also enables the NMDP to establish itself as an organization that is best-in-class on Social Responsibility, as it is working hard to solve this challenging social issue.

Once the potential donors are emotionally attached, they like to understand that they are interacting with a legitimate organization that has the authority to solve this problem. This is where the NMDP convinces them of its Brand value. The NMDP's association with the federal government and its affiliation with local, national and international organizations provide it the required Brand value on this subject. A certain portion of its marketing materials is targeted towards educating donors about NMDP and its practices; volunteers use this information during local events to educate potential donors about the NMDP Brand and make them feel comfortable about sharing their information. Using this approach, the NMDP delivers a best-in-class Brand-related customer experience.

Next, it makes it Convenient for donors to register in the program. The form requires minimum contact information from the donor to make it easy for them to register. Before April 2006, a blood draw by a registered medical practitioner was the only means to collect genetic information from donors. This was highly inconvenient for donors, and subsequently, some of them did not complete the registration process. The need for a medical practitioner to be present for the blood draw also restricted the number of marrow drives.

In April 2006, the NMDP introduced the cheek swab method, where the donor rubs a cotton swab on the inside of the cheek for ten seconds to collect the required genetic information. This new method made it Convenient and painless for donors to complete the registration. This also cleared the way for more marrow drives, as a medical practitioner was no longer required, and enabled the NMDP to register donors using social media and mail. Potential donors who showed interest in the program on social media would receive a package that contained the proper forms and a couple of cotton swabs; the donor would rub the swabs on inside of the cheek to collect the genetic information, fill out the forms, and mails both back to the NMDP, who would then enter the donor's contact genetic information into a secure database. By making it easy for the donor to register, the NMDP delivers a best-in-class customer experience on the Convenience factor.

Last but not the least, the NMDP assures donors that their information is secure and will not be shared with anyone, except in the case of a match. The NDMP also assures them that they will not be spammed, except for a yearly flyer requesting them to update their contact information. The data security and no-spam policy deliver a best-in-class Quality experience.

The NMDP delivers a best-in-class customer experience on four factors — Social Responsibility, Brand, Convenience and Quality — to its donors; the rest of the factors are not relevant in this particular case.

Customer Experience for Network Partners and Recipients

Finding and registering donors is just one part of the challenge for the NMDP; the other aspect is managing the network of partners involved in this eco-system. These include transplant centers, donor centers, collection centers, hospitals and others who help the NMDP throughout the search, match and transplant process.

The customer experience delivered by the NMDP to its network partners and recipients is shown in Figure 19.

When a patient is in need of a marrow transplant, this network of partners gathers patient information and provides it to the NMDP, which uses it to find a match from its huge database. It is the job of this partner network to work

Figure 19: Customer Experience Delivered by the NMDP to Its Partner Network

with the NMDP on behalf of patients, which they do many times a year, for finding a perfect match; which is Requirements-related customer experience.

To deliver a best-in-class customer experience on the Requirements factor, the NMDP needs to find that perfect match from its huge database. The perfect match is a donor who has a genetic match with the recipient, is physically fit to donate bone marrow, understands the donation/transplant process and is willing to go through the donation process.

The NMDP has been investing in developing a better and more accurate matching algorithm. The improvements to the algorithm are focused on improving the speed with which an accurate match can be found. Once a match is found in the database, NMDP does not pass it along to its partner networks; rather, it follows a process of further refining the match to ensure that it is perfect.

There is a long process that takes place after the potential donor is found, which begins with contacting the donor and conducting further tests to confirm the match. About 1 in 40 members are called in for this additional testing to determine if they are the best match for the patient; about 1 in 300 are selected and go through information sessions about the transplantation process. If they agree to continue, they undergo additional physical examinations to make sure that donation is safe for both patient and donor. After all the testing and education sessions, about 1 in 540 donors actually donate to the patient[42]. The rigor that NMDP puts into finding the perfect match ensures that it delivers a best-in-class customer experience on the Requirements factor to the patients and to their healthcare providers.

On average, the entire process, from finding the match to conducting the transplant, can take about 96 days, and in my friend's case he did not have enough time for it to complete. A significant portion of the 10,000 patients who need a transplant either do not find a match, or do not survive the time it takes for the process to complete. Because of this, the NMDP delivers a subpar customer experience on the Availability factor of customer experience.

The NMDP is making a significant technology investment to improve its matching algorithm, and thus the time it takes to complete the match-to-transplant process. It has already reduced the time by 15 percent by using online platforms to keep track of donors and recipients during the transplant process[43].

---

[42] National Marrow Donor Program (NMDP) facts and Figures
http://marrow.org/News/Media/Facts_and_Figures_(PDF).aspx
[43] FastCompany The World's most innovative 50 companies: For matching technology with critical transplant needs by Tara Moore & David Lidsky
http://www.fastcompany.com/most-innovative-companies/2012/national-marrow-donor-program

This will make it convenient for network partners, donors and recipients to keep track of the process and reduce the average time taken; this, in turn, will help the NMDP provide better Service/Support to both recipients and donors, as it will be able to provide accurate information throughout the process.

The NMDP hopes to find matches for all cases and cut down match-to-transplant process time by 25 percent by 2015; at that point it would deliver a better customer experience on the Availability factor.

The NMDP coordinates all the efforts required in finding the right donors and connecting the patient's healthcare professionals with the donor. This makes it Convenient for healthcare professionals to find a match through the NMDP. It is also making a technology investment to improve the Convenience factor of the customer experience; today the NMDP delivers an ordinary customer experience across the Convenience factor, but the technology investment could improve the overall experience.

Due to the size of its database and its affiliation with federal government and various local, national, international organizations, the NMDP has developed a strong Brand position in the industry, delivering a best-in-class customer experience on this factor. Due to its rigorous process of finding the perfect match for the patient, it delivers a best-in-class customer experience on the Quality factor as well.

One factor of the customer experience that is important to the transplant recipients, but is not under the NMDP's control, is the cost of each transplant — the Price factor of the customer experience. A bone marrow transplant is a very expensive procedure, where costs could range anywhere between $150,000 to $200,000[44]. Depending on insurance coverage and the number

---

[44] nbmtLINK Common Questions http://www.nbmtlink.org/common_questions/index.htm

of people who were tested for a match, the cost of finding a donor could vary as well, so there is no standard price that a recipient could expect to pay for the transplant. Because of this, the recipient's experience on the Price factor is subpar, which is not necessarily the experience that the NMDP wants to deliver. In fact, in 2011, the NMDP paid $2.2 million to qualifying patients through its Be The Match Foundation® Patient Assistance Program to cover some of the financial costs.

The National Marrow Donor Program (NMDP) is the biggest hope for patients who need bone marrow transplants. Hopefully, their technology investments will pay off and we won't lose any more friends or family members to this deadly disease.

In the next section, let me clarify the differences between the Availability and Convenience aspects of customer experience. If you refer back to Chapter 2 on the Customer Experience Framework, you will see that the Availability factor is about the customer having access to your product or service when they need it the most, whereas Convenience is about the ease of use of your product or service. Many of the examples throughout this book have highlighted the differences between these two factors, but to make it even more clear, let us look at another example.

Availability vs. Convenience

Have you ever tried losing weight? If so, then you know that it is a difficult challenge, as it requires habitual and behavioral changes that most people find difficult to make. Additionally, many of the judgments that you make on a daily basis are made without having the right information about the calories you are ingesting make it challenging to lose weight. For example, you want to eat right and work out; during your workout, you get enough information like the amount of calories you are burning, the number of miles you are running, and the time you have spent on the workout. But when it comes to eating right, it is very difficult to measure the calories that you are consuming, so you tend to make a judgment call based on what you like to eat and how full you feel. Your mind is not focused on changing the behaviors, so it finds reasons to justify that big burger, fries and soda. Not eating right after a workout does not help your cause, and you tend to maintain or even gain weight.

One solution to this problem can be found at MyFitnessPal.com, a website that focuses on helping people count calories and lose weight. It also has free apps that work on most types of cell phones, in addition to the online site. According to Google AdWords research, women between 25 and 44 are the biggest users of this calorie-counter website, which has close to 2.2 million worldwide unique visitors a month. They have almost 250,000 reviews on the Apple iTunes store, with an overall rating of 4.5 stars. When compared to other calorie-counting fitness-oriented apps, MyFitnessPal is clearly a success story.

MyFitnessPal's app is best-in-class at doing one thing: calculating the net calories consumed in a day, which are those consumed by eating food minus those that are burned off by exercising. The app has an extensive database of over a million foods, with detailed calorie counts for each type. For example, you can find the calorie count for all items on the McDonald's menu and the Subway menu, the salad that you pick up at Costco, or the organic fruits that you purchase at Whole Foods. Calorie information for a wide range of snacks, candy, chips and soda are also available. A separate database outlines the number of calories burned while engaging in an activity; so, for example, if you are leisure biking under 10 miles per hour for 30 minutes, you'll burn around 160 calories, whereas exercising on an elliptical trainer for 30 minutes burns 360 calories. Based on the food you eat and the exercise you do, this application tracks your net caloric intake during the day and helps you stay on your weight loss plan.

Let me share my experience of losing weight using the MyFitnessPal app. At the beginning I set myself a goal of losing 10 pounds over a period of four weeks; based on my current weight and my weight loss goal, I was given a daily net caloric intake goal by the app. Whenever I ate something, I would enter the calorie count of the food either by:

- Searching through the database for the food, and adding the quantity I consumed; once the food from the database was selected, it added all nutrition and calorie information to my daily diary.
- Scanning the bar code on packaged food using my smartphone's camera; the app read the bar code, found the food and added that calorie count to my daily diary.
- Manually adding the food calories to the daily diary, in cases where the food I ate was not available in the database.

Similarly, I was able to enter the calories burned by exercising into the app. Based on the calories consumed minus calories burned calculation, the app told me how many more calories I could consume for the rest of the day. It also showed me my projected weight at the end of the four weeks, which really motivated me to stay on track. The good news is that I did, in fact, meet my weight loss goal within that time.

Overall, the MyFitnessPal app is a great product, with a huge database of foods available that make it easy to find the right food and track the calories consumed.

What type of customer experience do you think this large database of food provides? Is it the Convenience-related customer experience or is it the Availability-related experience?

The large database, combined with a good user interface, delivers a best-in-class customer experience across the *Convenience* factor, as it makes it easy for the customer to find the right foods and to use the product effectively. Imagine if this product did not have such a massive database of foods: then I would have had to enter the calorie counts for most of the foods myself, making it considerably less convenient to use — especially since, in many cases, I wouldn't know the calorie count of what I was eating — so I would likely default to my old behavior of assuming that the big burger and fries do not contribute as many calories as they actually do to my diet. Given my weight loss goals, this would have been the wrong thing to do. It would make it inconvenient to use this app, and so I would stop using it. That's why this database has a big impact on the Convenience factor of customer experience.

It is unlikely that the database has any impact on the *Availability* factor of the customer experience because Availability is all about having access to a product at the time you need it most. In this cases, it would be a matter of having access to the app when I have data to enter. If I am not able to access the app when I need it the most, it would deliver poor customer experience on the Availability factor, and it would not matter if it had a massive database.

Having said that, though, MyFitnessPal delivers a best-in-class customer experience on the Availability factor as well, by offering its product on the web as well as across multiple mobile platforms like iPhone, Blackberry, and Android, ensuring that the customer has access to the product in a variety of ways.

Although MyFitnessPal delivers a best-in-class customer experience across both the Convenience and the Availability factors, the reasons for each are different. Hopefully, this example will help minimize any confusion you might have between the two.

Now let us see how the customer experience framework applies to innovations within the pharmaceutical industry. This industry has many different customers — the Food and Drug Administration (FDA), doctors, hospitals, insurers and patients — and they change their innovation focus based on which customers they are trying to serve. In the next chapter, we'll review a number of examples to understand how pharmaceutical companies shift their focus based on the current needs of those customers.

· CHAPTER 6 ·

Pharmaceutical Industry
Innovation

Social Responsibility-Focused Innovation

In the early 1980s, concern mounted about a new and deadly disease
called Acquired Immune Deficiency Syndrome (AIDS). It began spreading
fast among gay men, injection drug users and users of blood-related products, and quickly became a global epidemic. Many of the patients suffering
from this mysterious disease were falling ill to common viruses that would
not normally affect them — not only falling ill, but actually dying from these
ordinary ailments.

Since that time, the National Institutes of Health (NIH), the United States
government agency responsible for biomedical research — which spends
billions of dollars a year in conjunction with research universities, private
companies and internal researchers to understand how to detect, diagnose, prevent and cure diseases — has been funding research projects to
discover the characteristics of AIDS. Once they had demonstrated that

Human Immunodeficiency Virus (HIV) caused the disease, the NIH funded clinical research into drugs that could treat the HIV infection as well as clinical trials that would reveal drug combinations to help slow, prevent, and even eradicate the infection.

But when it began its mission, the NIH's primary focus was not to wipe out the disease, which at that time was considered incurable. There was no concern around determining the price points at which any drug might be sold, and certainly no focus on making a profitable blockbuster drug. The primary focus of the NIH at every stage was to provide a baseline cure that would enable physicians to slow the progress of AIDS and its impact on our society.

Who was the target customer for NIH-funded research? Not the patients or doctors who needed the medicine, as they had no clue to what it should be; and not the insurance companies, who did not know what to pay for such a medicine. The NIH's target customer was the federally-mandated Food and Drug Administration (FDA), the agency responsible for ensuring the safety of drugs before approving their release on the market.

Knowing your target customer is, not surprisingly, essential to effectively applying the customer experience framework outlined earlier. The pharmaceutical industry, the focus of this chapter, provides us with an opportunity to see how customer experience-focused innovation can be applied in a complex environment where the identity of the customer can vary widely.

From regulatory bodies like the FDA to doctors responsible for treating patients; from individuals who use the drugs to insurance companies that ultimately pay for them — all of these groups can be "customers" of the pharmaceutical industry at different points in time. In this chapter, we evaluate how the industry changes its innovation focus based on the customer experience it is trying to deliver to its target customer.

How do pharmaceutical companies deliver good customer experience to all of these players? By shifting their innovation focus to the needs of their target customer segment, and then by delivering the right customer experience to that customer. We will now explore three different examples where the innovation focus shifts based on the target customer type.

Returning to the example of NIH-funded research that was targeting the FDA, most institutions working on an AIDS cure were aware that the FDA had the Social Responsibility of providing a baseline cure for this rampant pandemic that threatened millions of people throughout the world. To meet its social obligation, the FDA trusted the NIH and its research partners to find a baseline cure for the disease.

The FDA expected a best-in-class customer experience on the Social Responsibility factor, as it wanted its research partners to figure out best ways to slow the progress of the disease. It relied on NIH-funded research to deliver this innovation, with the expectation that the NIH would do a good job at funding the right partners to find the cure — hence, it expected a best-in-class customer experience on the Brand factor. Moreover, the FDA's initial Requirements were to find a cure that slows down the progress of the disease. This Requirement had to be met for the FDA to approve the drug, so it expected a best-in-class customer experience on the Requirements factor. The customer experience expectation of the FDA is shown in Figure 20.

But why was the expectation subpar on the remaining six factors, especially Quality? Because the FDA's initial focus was not to eliminate the pandemic, but to take the right steps in slowing the impact of the HIV infection. It needed to act fast to approve drugs, even if they had minimal impact on HIV infection. This meant that the FDA was willing to overlook some Quality issues if the drug proved promising enough to lessen the impact

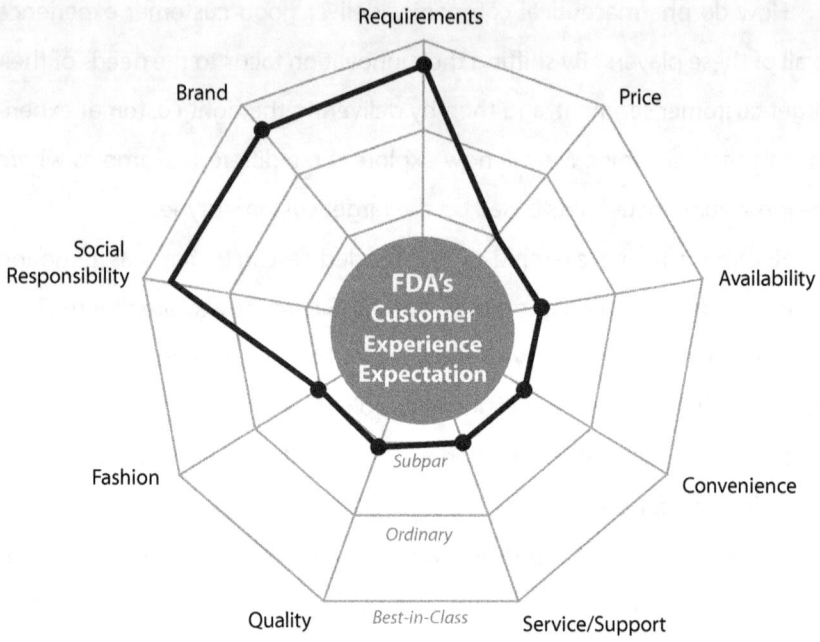

Figure 20: The FDA's Customer Experience Expectation for
Initial AIDS Drug Research

of this disease. Moreover, the FDA wanted to make the drug available to a contained population of AIDS patients, so that it could further understand its impact. This understanding, and the further evaluation of the drug, would enable the NIH and its research companies to improve on the drug and ultimately deliver a viable cure for the disease. Since the FDA was not looking to make the drug available to a larger population, its customer experience expectation on Availability was subpar. Price, Convenience, Service/Support, Fashion — none of these factors were important as the FDA kept working with the NIH and its research partners to find a cure for AIDS.

Once the baseline cure for HIV infection was achieved, the FDA, the NIH, research institutes and private companies would keep pushing the envelope further and innovating all types of drugs to prevent and slow the impact of AIDS, while delivering different customer experiences to different customers; but the initial customer experience was focused on Social Responsibility.

Convenience-Focused Innovation

Imagine you were prescribed a medicine that was to be taken three times a day. You plan on taking the first dose at 8 a.m., right before leaving for work; the second dose at 4 p.m.; and the last at midnight. You regularly take the first dose, but the second, is hard to remember as you might be in the middle of a meeting or busy doing something else at work. So you miss the scheduled time, and take the second dose sometime later in the day, and you almost always miss the third dose, as you are tired from the day's work and do not want to get out of bed. Taking the medicine thrice a day is highly inconvenient, which makes you skip doses and be non-compliant with the prescription. Now imagine that the dose was to be delivered through injection; the pain associated with administering the dose and the overall inconvenience associated with it will make you even more non-compliant. Let's see how the pharmaceutical industry solved this Convenience issue through innovation.

In the early 1980s, research on antidepressant drug called venlafaxine was being done at Wyeth's laboratories. Researchers were highly optimistic that this drug would deliver better results compared to those already present in the market. After a long period of testing and clinical trials, it was approved by FDA in early 1994. The drug was prescribed to be used twice a day to treat depression, general and social anxiety, and panic disorder.

Though the drug was very effective, it was difficult for doctors to force compliance with venlafaxine. Patients were usually ordered to take one dose in the morning and one in the evening, but as the effect of the morning dose started waning, they found it difficult to focus, and forgot to take the second dose. In social situations, they felt embarrassed to use the drug due to the fear of people finding about their medical condition, so even if the patient remembered to take their dose, they would only do so if they thought the environment was safe. Venlafaxine was also prescribed to children, who had to go to the nurse's station to take it, a process that was very embarrassing. This caused non-compliance for both adults and kids, and decreased the impact of the drug while prolonging the illness it was intended to treat.

Wyeth knew about this problem, and focused their research efforts on delivering the right customer experience to the patient population, which in this case was the target customer. The research led to an extended-release version of the same drug, called venlafaxine XR, which was a once-a-day dose. The dosage in this tablet was higher than the regular tablet, but was released over an extended period of time. In late 1997, the FDA approved venlafaxine XR, making it convenient for the customers to take their medicine once and not worry about their illness for rest of the day. Since the medicine was released over an extended period, the customer did not feel the effect of the medicine fading, and could carry on with their normal activities.

This also increased compliance with the medicine. The change in the customer experience between venlafaxine and venlafaxine XR is depicted in Figure 21.

So what is the difference in the customer experience delivered by venlafaxine and venlafaxine XR? It looks like the Brand, Requirements, Price, Availability and Quality factors did not change much between the two versions, but

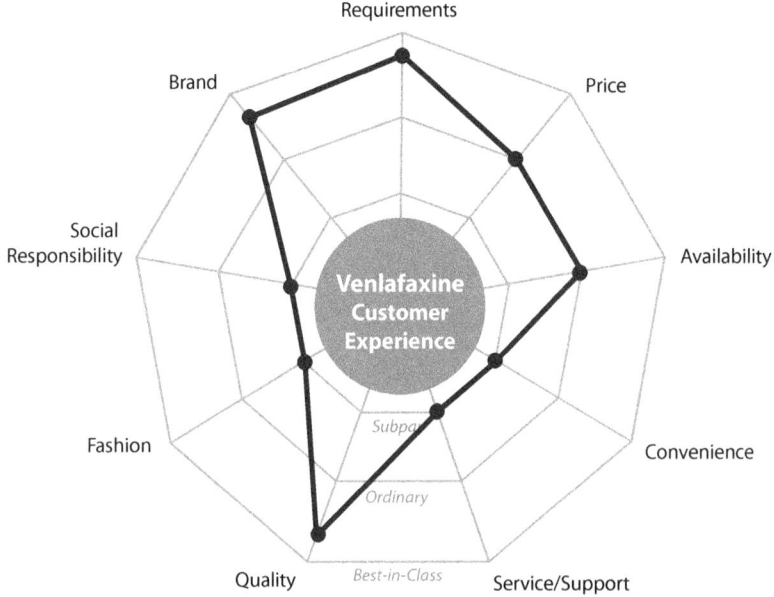

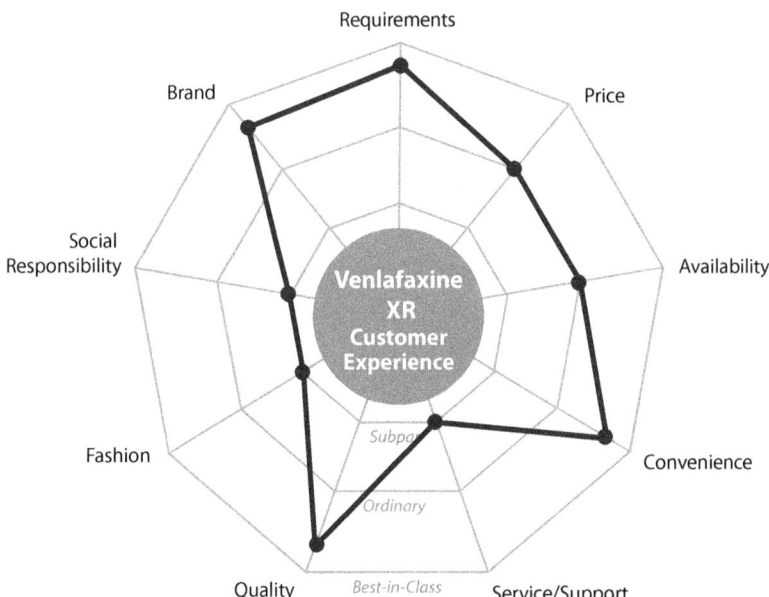

Figure 21: Comparison of the Venlafaxine and Venlafaxine XR Customer Experience

Convenience was the biggest change. By making the drug a once-a-day dose, it made it much more convenient for patients to take it, and increased their compliance, which in turn encouraged doctors to prescribe the drug. This approach to making venlafaxine convenient proved to be financially beneficial to Wyeth.

As the drug became more convenient to use, Wyeth realized that they could charge a significant premium for providing that Convenience. The allowed price for venlafaxine XR[45] was $123 for a 30-day supply; this was a 43 percent premium over a 30-day supply of regular venlafaxine.

Does the same formula of the same drug at a higher dosage released over an extended period deserve this kind of price premium? Apparently yes, as when presented with the option to use a once-a-day dosage or a twice-a-day dosage, patients usually preferred the former. Doctors also noticed the improved compliance of the once-a-day drug and preferred prescribing venlafaxine XR over venlafaxine.

Due to the high price premium and more doctors prescribing venlafaxine XR, the sales and profits for Wyeth increased significantly. In 2000, venlafaxine XR sales jumped by 64 percent, making it a billion-dollar drug. By 2007, it became the sixth-largest antidepressant drug on the market, with over 17 million prescriptions. These were amazing results, driven by customer convenience-focused innovation.

It is clear that patients and doctors liked the convenience and compliance provided by this drug. Did insurance companies like paying such high price premiums? During those boom years, when the economy was growing, they did not mind paying the premium for the extended-release drug, so it was a win-win situation for all involved in the ecosystem.

---

[45] Journal of Managed Care Pharmacy, Vol. 11, No. 9 published in November/December 2005

Another convenience-focused innovation in the pharmaceutical industry was the cure for osteoporosis. Researchers estimate that 1 out of 5 American women over the age of 50 have osteoporosis, a bone disease where the body fails to make new bone, as it is unable to absorb calcium from food. This causes fractures, further bone loss, and lots of pain. One drug that slows down the rate of bone loss and relieves pain is calcitonin. Initially, when this drug was formulated, it had to be injected into the body. It was highly inconvenient and painful for women to follow the required dosage, but to reduce pain levels and bone loss, they continued taking injections.

Calcitonin was a successful drug and sold about $15 to $20 million per year. Then Novartis invented a nasal spray version of calcitonin, and this completely changed the customer experience for women suffering from osteoporosis. Now they did not have go through the pain and inconvenience of injections; they could just inhale the medicine once a day. This changed the fortunes for Novartis, as calcitonin became a $700 million drug.

Such success stories motivated a lot of customer convenience-focused innovation in the pharmaceutical industry. Many of the existing drugs were released in once-a-day dosages, with huge price premiums. In May 2002, the National Institute for Health Care Management (NIHCM) announced that 61 percent of the increase in 2001 pharmacy sales was contributed by Price increase, and about 24 percent of the total pharmacy sales were attributable to the shift to higher-cost drugs like venlafaxine XR.

This alarmed insurance companies, and they started questioning the benefit of once-a-day drugs. They also questioned the huge price premium for the same drug without any improvement in efficacy (the impact of a drug on a disease). Many stopped reimbursement for extended-release drugs, which forced doctors to prescribe regular versions of those drugs.

But patient expectations had changed already, as they had become used to taking once-a-day doses and did not want to go back to multiple doses. So they pushed back against the insurance companies, who in turn pushed back against the pharmaceutical companies to improve efficacy of the drugs.

"Insurers, as a customer type, got used to the convenience, and they wanted a lot more from the pharmaceutical industry; they wanted more efficacy," said Dr. Purnanand Sarma, president and CEO of Taris Biomedical during an interview.

This changed the focus of pharmaceutical industry innovation to the payers' — that is, the insurance companies' — customer experience. The industry's innovation focus shifted from convenience to convenience plus efficacy. Once-a-day dosage molecules became the norm, and more emphasis was placed on improving the overall efficacy of the drug. Let me give you one more example of the impact of change in the customer experience focus to efficacy: the Requirements of the drug.

Requirements-Focused Innovation

Consider a virus that keeps replicating itself within a patient's body, every minute of every hour of every day. After reaching certain levels, every replication of the virus is more harmful to the patient, and reduces their ability to fight the virus. If this replication is not stopped, it could cause severe damage or even kill the patient.

One such virus is hepatitis C, which causes infectious liver diseases. This infection is caused due to intravenous drug use, poorly sterilized medical equipment, and blood transfusions. Chronic hepatitis C can cause liver cancer, liver failures or other deadly diseases. One of the characteristics of the hepatitis C virus is that it replicates itself and keeps growing in the patient's body, while the patient's immune system loses its ability to fight the virus, thus patients suffering from hepatitis C need a strong drug that not only stops it from growing, but also improves the immune system's ability to fight it.

This is where interferon a protein that is capable of interfering with hepatitis C virus replication, comes in. In drug form, patients inject it once every day to restrict the replication of the virus, but there are significant problems with interferon.

For one, injecting any drug on a daily basis is not a great experience; it is painful and disruptive to patients' lives. For another, as the day progresses, the effect of the drug starts to decrease, and the virus that was constrained up until that point starts replicating again, making it difficult for the drug to overcome it. Imagine a duel of equals, where each combatant delivered the right number of blows to the opponent and survived for one more round; during the day, interferon would beat up on the virus, and at night, the virus would replicate again and regain its strength.

Apart from not being convenient, this drug also did not meet the Requirements or Quality aspects of the customer experience of the patients. From the insurance company's perspective, interferon did not provide a lot of value, but nevertheless, it was a drug that could slow virus replication.

This is where convenience plus efficacy-focused innovation comes in, with the addition of further drugs to interferon to help it stay in the body longer. This longer-lasting version of the fighter drug is called pegylated interferon. The advantage of this version is that it only needs to be injected once a week, as it maintains interferon concentration levels in the body for seven days. During this longer period of time, it slows down the replication of the virus and strengthens the immune system in order to fight the virus.

Imagine our duel again, only this time the drug is much stronger and lasts much longer. So the daily turn of fortunes between drug and virus does not happen, and before its potency fades, the patient injects the next dose of pegylated interferon, and further strengthens the ability to fight the virus.

The customer experiences for interferon and pegylated interferon are shown in Figure 22.

With this innovation, patients have had much better outcomes in terms of fighting the hepatitis C virus, and in a convenient way.

This innovation is a huge success with both patients and payers, as it is not only convenient but it also improves the efficacy of the drug. This was possible because the Requirements of the drug were modified. Now, the Requirement of the drug is not only to restrict the replication of the virus, but also to stay in the body longer and deliver the benefits over a longer period of time.

Changing Focus of Innovation

If we put together the examples of AIDS, venlafaxine XR and pegylated interferon, what similarities or differences do we observe?

Let us analyze the similarities first. All these are examples of customer experience-focused innovation, where the end result is to deliver an experience important to the customer. With AIDS research, it was about Social Responsibility-focused innovation to find a, baseline cure for a deadly pandemic. Venlafaxine XR was about improving customer convenience and in turn, increasing patient compliance. Pegylated interferon was about delivering more convenience and better efficacy.

Another common characteristic across all the three examples is that companies were able to demand significant Price premiums for these

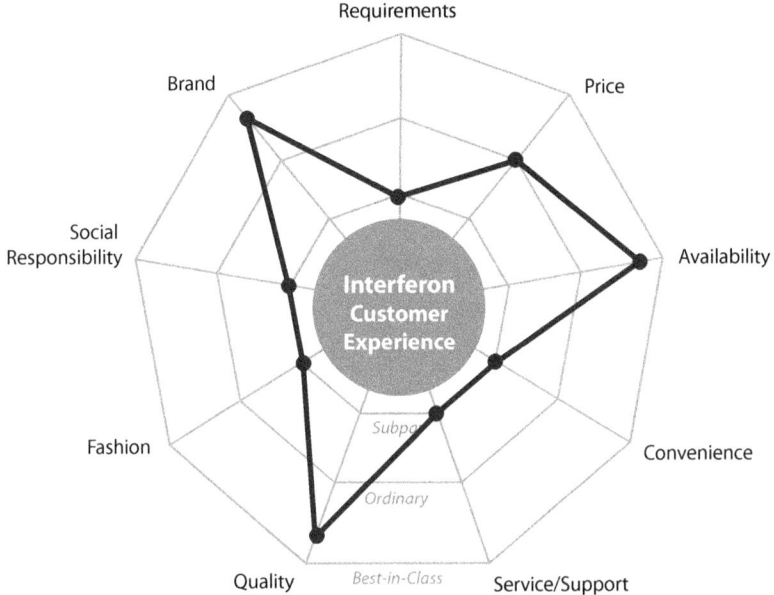

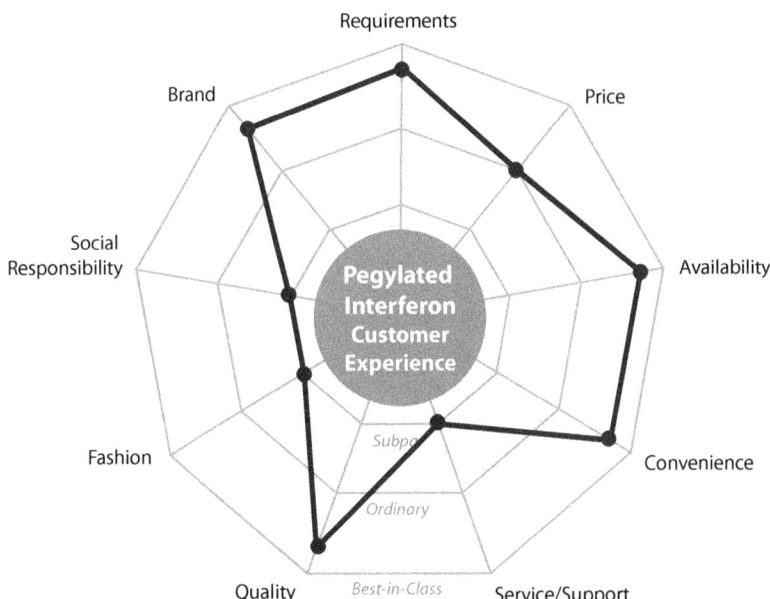

Figure 22: Comparison of the Interferon and Pegylated Interferon Customer Experiences

innovations, and at the same time able to sell more of the drugs, making it financially rewarding for their innovators.

Now what do you think the differences are between these examples? If you thought it was the customer type, you are right, as it changed throughout the examples. For AIDS research, the customer type was the regulators who had the Social Responsibility to approve a baseline cure. For venlafaxine XR, the customer type was patients looking for a convenient dosage, and doctors who wanted to increase drug compliance. For pegylated interferon, the customer type was insurance companies, who were demanding better results for their money, and patients, who were demanding more convenience.

As the customer types changed, so too did the innovation focus of the pharmaceutical industry. They were focused on delivering the customer experience that mattered to the target customer, and by doing that, they were successful with their innovations and in positively shifting their financial fortunes.

The key, then, is to know your target customer segment, know the kind of customer experience they want, and deliver that customer experience by innovating.

Up until now, you have seen customer experience-focused innovation work in a diverse set of industries and help innovators shift the market away from incumbents. In the next chapter, we will look at different types of innovations and see how customer experience-focused innovation fits. This will help you think through the methods in which *you* can shift the markets in your favor.

· CHAPTER 7 ·

Delivering a Best-In-Class
Customer Experience

From Netflix's disruption of the movie rental business to Big Pharma's innovative approach to developing extended-release medicines, all the examples I've shared with you have resulted in huge shifts in markets, often toppling seemingly unbeatable market leaders. This enabled the newcomers to sustain a considerable strategic advantage that other companies failed to imitate.

So how might you use this knowledge to shift *your* industry or market? More specifically, what can these disruptors teach us about how to innovate in a way that can be adapted to your unique situation?

As you can see from Figure 23 below, every company I've discussed has leveraged one or more kinds of innovation: Business Model Innovation, Process Innovation, or Product Innovation. Let's first review what we mean by each of these innovation types, before exploring which ones best align with the superior customer experience you want to deliver.

	Requirements	Price	Convenience	Availability	Service/ Support	Quality	Fashion	Social Responsibility
Business Model Innovation	"M-Pesa"	"Netflix" "Southwest Airlines" "Amazon. com Prime"	"Challenger Corp"		"Zappos"	"BMW"		
Process Innovation	"NMDP"	"M-Pesa"	"Netflix" "NMDP" "M-Pesa"	"Netflix"	"Zappos"	"Toyota"	"Fab.com"	"Interface Carpet" "NMDP
Product Innovation	"iPhone" "Sonosite" "Pegylated Interferon" "M-Pesa"	"M-Pesa"	"Venlafaxine XR" "MyFitness Pal" "Blood Glucometer"	"Netflix"			"Motorola RAZR"	"AIDS Medicine"

Figure 23: Customer Experience and Different Types of Innovation

Business Model Innovation

This type of innovation deals with different methods of delivering products or services to the customer, while profiting from doing so. A 2008 article in the *Harvard Business Review* by Clay Christensen and his colleagues on "Reinventing the Business Model" noted that 11 of the 27 companies that made it to the *Fortune* 500 list in the last decade had done it through business model innovation[46].

To understand this type of innovation better, consider the example of

[46] Reinventing Your Business Model by Mark W. Johnson, Clayton M. Christensen, and Henning Kagermann; Harvard Business Review, The Magazine, December 2008

Gillette's innovation of the razor industry. To shift the market away from its competitors, Gillette started giving away cheap razors in hopes of making more profits on the blades. This model worked very well, as it locked in the customers who had who had bought Gillette razors and were therefore committed to buying their blades.

As an alternative example, consider the "as a Service" models we often see nowadays. This could be "Software as a Service", "Platform as a Service", "Infrastructure as a Service", or many other variations. The innovation in this type of business model is built around the product delivery method and the way the customer is charged.

Let us look at how Salesforce.com uses the Software-as-a-Service (SaaS) model. Traditionally, when customers purchased software, they hosted it in their own data center and maintained it using their own staff. They then pay an annual maintenance fee to get the latest updates, which they install themselves. The SaaS model changed that completely. With Salesforce.com, customers pay for the use of software on a subscription basis, either monthly or annual, and Salesforce.com is responsible for hosting, maintaining and updating it. The advantage to the customer is that they can enjoy access to the software after paying the subscription fee, without having to be concerned with maintaining it or cutting large checks for an upfront purchase.

Not surprisingly, many companies have enjoyed huge success by adopting business model innovations.

Process Innovation

Walmart shifted the entire retail industry in its favor by using process innovation. To become the low price leader in a thin-margin retail industry,

Walmart had to be very efficient with its cost structure. It found there were significant expenses in warehousing and transportation that it could minimize to gain that strategic advantage. Before adopting process innovation, Walmart had half-full trucks running from warehouse to store locations and products sitting too long in the warehouse, all of which impacted their transportation and product costs.

Walmart decided to implement a cross-docking process to minimize these operational costs. This meant that a Walmart store could place an order for a product whenever it was running low on stock, and the supplier would deliver the product to Walmart's distribution center, where it would be moved quickly into a truck scheduled to leave for the store. Only when all products ordered by that particular store arrived and the truck was full, was it dispatched.

Process innovation, in a simplistic form, is about how a company operates to deliver the customer experience desired by its customers. It could be a behind-the-scenes process, as in the case of Walmart using a cross-docking process to lower its operational costs so it can continue to offer lower prices, or it could be a process experienced by the customer as they do business with the company. In a nutshell, process innovation enables companies to improve their operational execution, which in turn helps deliver the desired customer experience.

To cite another example, Southwest Airlines needed to cut down their costs in order to offer lower prices to customers. They succeeded by purchasing only Boeing 737s, and developing all their operational processes and knowledge base around this one type of aircraft. Since keeping their planes flying is what makes an airline money, they implemented process innovations like open seating that enabled passengers to board planes faster, and minimized Southwest's time on the ground.

In both of these cases, process innovation was the "secret sauce" that made it extremely difficult for Walmart and Southwest's competitors to imitate or best them.

Product Innovation

This type of innovation deals with either incrementally improving product performance or totally disrupting a product category with never-before-seen capabilities.

Apple's iPhone was a disruptive product innovation that totally changed the way people used their cell phones, by allowing consumers to browse the internet in a way that had not been possible before. iPhone was incrementally better in the ability to make calls and data speeds supported by the phone, which is incremental innovation.

Similarly, Sonosite created a product that was not existent in the market before with the Hand-Carried Ultrasound (HCU) system. They were funded by DARPA to innovate and create this system so it could used on battlefields. Sonosite had experience in traditional ultrasound machine development, and figured out ways to deliver similar technology in a much smaller form. They were successful in shrinking the technology using Application Specific Integrated Circuits (ASIC), computer chips created to perform very specific tasks, and they eliminated many complex features from traditional ultrasound machines to make it easy to use. This product innovation by Sonosite engineers is a combination of disruptive and incremental innovation.

Delivering Customer Experience Through Innovation

Any or all of these three types of innovation could help your company shift the market in your favor. In fact, employing just one of them might not be enough; you might require a combination of innovation types in order to help you deliver a best-in-class customer experience, according to the nine key factors introduced in Chapter Two and outlined throughout this book.

So how do you understand which type of innovation is required, and where to focus your resources? First, you should focus on the customer experience that you would like to deliver and its underlying factors. Once you understand this, then focus on the types of innovation that are going to deliver that experience.

In order to demonstrate how this is achieved, let's look more deeply at the way some companies we explored in Chapters Three through Six have used different types of innovation to deliver the desired customer experience in their respective markets.

I'll begin with the simplest example: ChallengerCo's market shift across a single factor — Convenience — using business model innovation. Then I'll outine how Zappo's drew on process innovation to help them deliver best-in-class Service/Support to their customers. This will be followed by the product innovation done in the pharmaceutical industry to deliver best-in-class Convenience and Requirements experience. Finally, I'll show you how Netflix drew on all three types of innovation to topple Blockbuster, by delivering a superior customer experience across the Convenience, Availability, and Price factors.

ChallengerCo's Innovation

Remember in Chapter Four, when I outlined how ChallengerCo had introduced their own subscription-based model to take over market share in the networking equipment industry? ChallengerCo wanted to deliver a best-in-class customer experience on the Convenience factor. To deliver this customer experience, it created a subscription program for its networking equipment, which was a business model innovation. This was a risky move, however, as it had to use its line of credit to finance the purchase of equipment and then provide it to customers on a subscription basis. Since the customers had no contracts, they could return the equipment at any time without penalties.

Imagine the level of risk this business model posed to the company. On the one hand, it could take market share from the leader and beat them at their own game; on the other hand, it could have ended up with huge debt and returned equipment. The business model innovation that ChallengerCo embraced was to balance risk against the rewards while designing the program. They had to consider many different factors before offering the program to its customers, and built detailed models that helped predict likely future scenarios in detail, including financial models looking at credit exposure risk and revenue uplift. The modeling showed the financial risks of this program were not severe, so they could afford to offer the program.

What if customers had returned equipment frequently to replace them with newer equipment? In this case, ChallengerCo could have ended up with large inventory of returned equipment. To understand the impact of this risk, ChallengerCo interviewed customers to understand how easy it was for them to return the equipment. They found that it was extremely inconvenient for a customer to remove and return their networking equipment, as this would lead to network outages and disruption of their day-to-day business. Furthermore, networking staff did not believe in disturbing a well-functioning network, so they would not remove the equipment just to replace it with something newer. Based on their interviews, ChallengerCo concluded that there wasn't as much risk in adopting this model as they had originally anticipated.

The subscription program, its terms, and the related pricing model were the business model innovations that enabled the ChallengerCo to deliver a customer experience that was unique and best-in-class. This was something that the market leader could not imitate, as its model was based on selling the equipment today and pocketing all the revenue immediately. It had the largest market share with this model. Adopting a subscription model would mean that they could not have pocketed all the revenue at once, but it would have to take monthly payments over the years. This was not attractive to the market leader, as for them, revenue today is better than promise of revenue tomorrow. While ChallengerCo did not have that immediate revenue, it was willing to take the promise of revenue over a longer period.

Zappos.com Innovation

Let us look at one more process innovation example, to further understand the impact of this type of approach. Zappos.com's main claim to fame is delivering best-in-class Service/Support to its customers, and they do many things to achieve that. But to understand their process innovation, let us look at the instant shipping policy they follow.

Early on, Zappos.com realized that they could not just take orders and rely on sellers to fulfill them. This is because if the seller did not deliver the product on time, it would deliver a bad customer experience that would reflect poorly on Zappos.com. So to control the entire experience, Zappos.com opened a warehouse and stocked every pair of shoes it sold on its website. It had no experience in managing this huge volume of inventory, and needed to find a way to identify the right pair of shoes in a short amount of time in order to meet their order fulfillment promise.

The company experimented with different internal processes to ensure that they would be able to find the right shoe when an order was placed, but without much success. Finally, it invented its own licensing system for managing the shoes. Using this process, each pair of shoes is assigned a license number, which is scanned into the system along with the location where it is stocked. When a customer places an order, the employee working on fulfilling that order knows the exact location of that exact pair of shoes, so they do not need to search for them; they can pick them up as soon as the order is placed and ship it to the customer.

This type of process innovation helps Zappos.com deliver the right customer experience, but the customer never sees the process that is hard at work behind the scenes.

Pharmaceutical Industry Innovation

In Chapter Six, on pharmaceutical industry innovation, we saw that pharmaceutical companies focused on developing extended-release versions of drugs. These versions made it convenient for the patient to follow the dosage and led to increased compliance. How did the companies achieve the capability of releasing the drug over an extended period of time instead of immediate release?

Controlled-release technology for drugs had been in existence since the 1960s, but it was not perfect. A zero-order release mechanism was required in which the drug release rate was independent of time and the concentration of drug remaining the body. This was challenging to achieve, as with time drugs lost their ability to keep up their concentration levels. This is when the Alza Corporation invented the osmotic-controlled release oral delivery system (OROS), in which a very small hole (100 to 120 microns in size) is drilled into the tablet using a laser. As the tablet enters the body, water passes through the tablet and pushes the drug out through this hole. Given the small size of the hole, the drug is released slowly over a period of time. This was a great innovation, as it transformed drug delivery systems and enabled a zero-order release mechanism. This, along with a few other mechanisms, became the foundation for extended-release drugs. It was a great product innovation, as it changed the way the product worked and enabled once-a-day dosage, making it convenient for users to follow the dosage and achieve compliance.

Netflix's Innovation

Now let us see how Netflix used all three types of innovation to deliver a desired customer experience. As you saw in Chapter Three, through experimentation, Netflix found that delivering a better customer experience across the Convenience, Availability and Price factors helped it topple the Blockbuster giant and become #1.

So how did Netflix manage to do this, and what did they innovate? Their business model was based on mailing DVDs to customers using the postal service. They did not invent the DVD, and they were certainly not in charge of the postal service; their unique contribution was to connect the two together. But what was so innovative about this, and how was Netflix able to sustain its leadership position? To understand this, let us peel the onion further and see how Netflix innovated to deliver a best-in-class customer experience.

First, consider the Price factor. Netflix introduced the flat-fee subscription model, where the price paid by the customer was independent of the number of movies they watched. Up until that time, customers paid a fee for each individual rental, but with the new model, they were able to watch any number of movies without having to worry about rental or late fees. They could, for example, hold on to a single movie for a month, or rent a different one every day, and still pay the same flat fee.

To deliver this best-in-class customer experience, Netflix had to take a lot of risks. To start with, it did not know the impact of this model on its financials. If done right, the model could lead to profitable growth, but if things didn't turn out the way they expected, they'd likely face bankruptcy. To understand this further, consider the cost of purchasing and mailing DVDs; if the subscription model was successful, then Netflix would have to purchase enough discs to meet the customer demand — a significant financial burden. It could also lead to high mailing costs if the majority of customers used Netflix as a daily rental service, as there would be a high volume of discs being mailed back and forth. In this situation, it would be difficult for Netflix to be profitable.

Even though the subscription model was risky, Netflix launched the model and shifted the market away from the incumbents.

Is Netflix's flat-fee subscription model truly an innovation, or just a pricing tactic? I think it is business model innovation, as it took much more than just a pricing change to implement and be successful. It involved changing the way the product was delivered — mail instead of in-store pickup — and how customers paid for the product, with a monthly subscription instead of pay-per-rental.

In fact, this business model innovation was not at all easy for the giant Blockbuster to imitate. After all, they had made billions of dollars from in-store, one-time rental revenues, and millions from late fees. By switching over to this flat fee, subscription-based model, they would have lost much of their rental revenue and all of their late fee revenue, so they did not want to imitate this model.

Did Netflix just innovate on the business model, or did it do more to deliver a best-in-class customer experience across the Price factor? It could not have achieved this goal with just business model innovation. It had to squeeze every penny out of its operations to make it financially viable to offer a flat-fee subscription. Therefore, they also needed process innovation to support their innovative business model.

To deliver a best-in-class experience on the Price aspect, Netflix had to be very cost effective, so much so that every penny that it reduced from of its operations made it financially viable for it to deliver the experience. What innovation helped it become most cost-effective with its operations?

Let us take a look at the Netflix mailing envelope, and see how it changed over the years. In 1999, it was made of cardboard and weighed much more than what it does today[47]. Though it was secure, and ensured that the DVD did not get damaged during shipping, it was not cost-efficient. Growth in the number of DVDs mailed led to an increase in mailing costs, and this led to the next generation of mailing envelopes, which were made out of thick paper. In these envelopes, DVDs were loaded at the top, but this was deemed

---

[47] CNN Money, The Evolution of Netflix Envelope By G Pascal Zachary, Business 2.0 Magazine; April 21, 2006 http://money.cnn.com/popups/2006/biz2/netflix/frameset.exclude.html

inconvenient so the next iteration was a side-loading envelope. Over the years, many experiments were conducted with the envelope — plastic envelopes to paper envelopes, top-loading to side-loading, unprinted envelopes to envelopes printed with advertisements, no bar codes to dual bar codes, and different mechanisms for using the same envelope for return mailing. Throughout the years, the focus for Netflix was to reduce mailing costs while making it convenient for the customer to use the same envelope to mail back a DVD. The envelope design also helped in improving mailing operations. The innovation around the mailing envelope is product innovation, as it helped Netflix deliver its service to, customers.

Next let us understand the innovation in internal operations for mailing and receiving the DVDs, and how that helped Netflix eliminate costs.

Every day, thousands of discs are delivered to Netflix's distribution centers by the postal service. Netflix's goal is to process every disc that it receives on the same day with minimal errors, as errors made in receiving, sorting and shipping of DVDs are expensive. It uses a combination of manual processes and automation to ensure that errors are minimized, and discs returned to the distribution center are processed quickly and mailed to the next customer.

The manual process deployed by Netflix guides the employees at the distribution center to follow the right steps in processing returned discs. They open the envelopes, scan the bar code on the disc sleeve, look for any customer notes, check to see if the disc is correct, clean it, make sure it is still playable, and inspect the label on the sleeve[48].

The work bench used by the employees is designed for the job they are performing. The work area has clear signs telling the workers what they need

---

[48] Business Inside; Here's How Netflix Sends You All Those DVDs by Jay Yarrow; http://www.businessinsider.com/netflix-shipping-2011-7#here-are-the-simple-rules-for-netflix-employees-1

to do and where they need to put processed discs. For example, there are "four steps to rental return" signs on the walls that tell the employees what they need to do with each return[49]. There are also clearly marked bins for placing customer notes, mismatches, and cracked discs. This ensures that employees are following the process designed to minimize errors in processing.

After checking the discs and scanning them into the system, the employees place them into stacks that are fed into a sorting machine which can sort 30,000 discs every hour into proper slots. Once all the sorting is complete, the mailing machine takes on the task of stuffing outgoing discs into envelopes and getting them ready for shipment. This machine can stuff up to 4,200 discs per hour into the envelopes. Once all the outgoing envelopes are ready, they are loaded into a truck that drops them off at the nearest post office. This automation ensures that the mailing of discs is cost-efficient and quick, with minimal errors.

These well-defined manual processes that reduce processing errors, and the automation for mailing discs, ensure that overall operations costs are lower — a form of process innovation. This enables Netflix to deliver a best-in-class customer experience on the Price factor.

Let us now see what type of innovation helped Netflix deliver a best-in-class customer experience on the Convenience factor. By definition, the Convenience factor requires Netflix to make it easier for the customer to rent movies. By delivering the DVDs to a customer's home, it ensures this customer experience. But it also does so by making it easier for the customer to pick the right DVD to rent. Netflix designed a predictive model, called Cinematch, that uses user ratings data to predict customer preferences. Netflix knew that

---

[49] Ibid

delivering a best-in-class experience on this factor was key to its success, so it launched an open competition with an award of one million dollars to anyone who could improve their Cinematch algorithm by more than 10 percent. As part of the training data set, Netflix provided over 100 million ratings from more than 400,000 users on over 17,000. Using this training data set, competitors could try to implement an algorithm that would be better than Cinematch in predicting user ratings. BellKor's Pragmatic Chaos team was able to improve the algorithm by 10.46 percent, and won the million-dollar award[50] This is product innovation, where the core product offering, in this case online presentation of movies based on user ratings, was improved using open innovation.

To deliver best-in-class customer experience on the Availability aspect, Netflix has to ensure that customers have a rental available when they are ready to watch it. It has to be very efficient and minimize the time it takes to get the next DVD to the customer.

The internal process of receiving, sorting and mailing discs on the same day adds to the Availability factor of customer experience delivered by Netflix. Customers can be sure that once the rental is mailed back, it will be processed quickly and the next rental will in the mail soon, so there are no unacceptable delays in watching the next movie in their queue, and some assurance that the disc isn't damaged or faulty.

To deliver a best-in-class customer experience on the Availability factor, Netflix also needs to reduce the time the rental discs spend in the mail. To achieve this goal, they have opened 58 distribution centers[51] across the

---

[50] Netflix Prize: http://en.wikipedia.org/wiki/Netflix_Prize
[51] Netflix Statistics by Statistics Brain http://www.statisticbrain.com/netflix-statistics/

country. This ensures that discs spend only one day in transit between the customer's home and the nearest Netflix distribution center.

Having these internal operations and distribution center networks in place are further examples of the process innovation that helps Netflix deliver the kind of customer experience it wants to deliver, at a competitive price point. This process innovation has become the strategic advantage for Netflix, and has helped ward off competitive threats to its market position, as it would be difficult and would require considerable financial investment for anyone to build a similarly large distribution network and internal operations with a one-day turnaround time, let alone try to improve on them.

Fitting It All Together

Now that we have reviewed examples of how different types of innovation were aligned with specific customer experience factors that these companies wanted to leverage, it's your turn!

To ensure this approach works for your company, you first need to be clear about where your future advantage lies. Are you most likely to shift the incumbent's market share by challenging them on Requirements, Price, Convenience, Availability, Service/Support, Quality, Fashion, Social Responsibility, or Brand? Once you have decided on that — and remember, you will typically need to excel in at least three of these factors, but not so many that you bankrupt yourself! — then it's time to examine which type of innovation (Business Model Innovation, Process Innovation, and/or Product Innovation) is best suited to your needs. The examples offered throughout this book will act as guides, depending on which industry or market you are looking to disrupt.

Here are some steps you could take to effectively use this framework in delivering a best-in-class customer experience.

Imagine you are an innovator at a company with an established customer base; you need to start with an internal assessment of the customer experience. Follow these steps to conduct the internal assessment:

- Educate all customer-facing employees about the customer experience and its benefits
- Give employees a broad definition of each of the nine factors
- Ask employees to assess the customer experience delivered by your company on each factor as being "best-in-class", "ordinary" or "subpar"
- Ask employees to assess the customer experience they believe is desired by the customers on each of the nine factors
- Aggregate the results and share them with the executives of your organization

This will provide you with a good starting point, as it shows the gap in the customer experience delivered by your company and the one your customer-facing employees believe is desired by the customers. Do not rely solely on the findings of the internal assessment, however, as your customers have not yet provided you with any input.

All innovators, with or without an established customer base, should reach out to their current and potential customers and make sure they understand their customer experience needs. This can be done by interviewing the customers, with a focus is on the job the customer is trying to do, and ways to make it easier. Make sure that you do not ask them directly about the factors on which they want a best-in-class experience, as they will ask for one on all factors. Instead, focus on what they are trying to accomplish, and how you can improve their overall experience on any factors.

One way I have found very effective in the B2B software industry is to "job-shadow" a customer. I would visit a customer, sit behind them and watch them do their work. They might or might not use my products during the time I am watching, but I nonetheless learn a lot about their needs just by observing them. I find out about all the products they use while doing their jobs, and the shortcuts they take to make their lives easier. This gives me a good sense of their pain points, and the opportunities for delivering a best-in-class customer experience.

Qualitative data from customer interviews and job-shadows will help you form an opinion about the customer experience desired. It is now time to get some quantitative data to support your qualitative analysis. You can also conduct structured surveys, which will provide you with quantitative data on the importance of the factors and customer satisfaction associated with each.

Once you are done gathering customer feedback, you should be able to figure out the gaps in the desired customer experience and make it your strategy to deliver a best-in-class customer experience to cover those gaps.

Once the strategy is finalized and you know the factors in which you are going to be best-in-class, communicate this information to all your employees. Make sure they understand the reasons behind this focus on customer experience and its benefits. This will ensure that the entire company is focused on the most important factors and delivers a best-in-class customer experience.

You should also make sure that all internal and external activities are geared towards delivering a best-in-class customer experience on the factors that you choose. For every new initiative that requires executive approval, ensure that executives test it to determine its impact on the appropriate customer experience factors. Approve only those initiatives that improve the customer experience on the most important factors.

The strategy, organization and process should focus your company on delivering a best-in-class customer experience on the most important factor, which will in turn ensure that you win the marketplace.

The fact is, opportunities are there for the taking. A focused organization that knows how to be best-in-class in delivering the right customer experience will shift the market. As relative newcomers like Netflix, ChallengerCo, Sonosite, and Hipcricket have demonstrated, giants can and will be toppled. The decision rests on whether or not you are prepared to apply the proven, best-in-class customer experience framework offered in this book, and have the desire and drive to become the new #1!

Index

ABOUT THE AUTHOR

Jagan Nemani is an innovation-focused executive who believes in developing innovative solutions to deliver a best-in-class customer experience. He has more than 14 years of experience encompassing product, process and business model innovations. His experience encompasses the software, telecom, semiconductor, insurance, cleantech and government procurement industries. He has successfully formulated and implemented game-changing strategies that have improved the top-line growth and bottom-line business performance of his clients. Based on years of experience and research for this book, he has developed an innovative customer experience framework that can be used to understand customers and deliver a best-in-class experience.

Jagan has an MBA (with honors) in strategic management and finance from University of Chicago, Booth School of Business. He has a master's degree in engineering, with a concentration in microelectronics, from the Birla Institute of Technology and Sciences in Pilani, India.

9 781477 579749